THE

W

WORD

**Witchcraft labelling
and child safeguarding
in social work practice**

Other books you may be interested in:

Anti-racism in Social Work Practice
Edited by Angie Bartoli ISBN 978-1-909330-13-9

Mental Health and the Criminal Justice System
Ian Cummins ISBN 978-1-910391-90-7

Modern Mental Health: Critical Perspectives on Psychiatric Practice
Edited by Steven Walker ISBN 978-1-909330-53-5

Observing Children and Families: Beyond the Surface
By Gill Butler ISBN 978-1-910391-62-4

Psychosocial and Relationship-based Practice
By Claudia Megele ISBN 978-1-909682-97-9

Social Media and Social Work Education
Edited by Joanne Westwood ISBN 978-1-909682-57-3

Understanding Substance Use: Policy and Practice
By Elaine Arnull ISBN 978-1-909330-93-1

What's Your Problem? Making Sense of Social Policy and the Policy Process
By Stuart Connor ISBN 978-1-909330-49-8

Titles are also available in a range of electronic formats. To order please go to our website www.criticalpublishing.com or contact our distributor NBN International, 10 Thornbury Road, Plymouth PL6 7PP, telephone 01752 202301 or email orders@nbninternational.com

THE

WORD

Witchcraft labelling and child safeguarding in social work practice

**Prospera Tedam
& Awura Adjoa**

First published in 2017 by Critical Publishing Ltd
Reprinted in 2018

British Library Cataloguing in Publication Data
A CIP record for this book is available from the British Library

ISBN: 978-1-912096-00-8

This book is also available in the following e-book formats:
MOBI ISBN: 978-1-912096-72-5
EPUB ISBN: 978-1-912096-71-8
Adobe e-book ISBN: 978-1-912096-70-1

Cartoons by Harry Venning
Cover design by Out of House
Text design by Greensplash Limited
Project management by Out of House Publishing
Printed an bound in Great Britain by 4edge, Essex

Critical Publishing
3 Connaught Road
St Albans
AL3 5RX
www.criticalpublishing.com

Paper from responsible sources

Contents

Meet the authors

Prospera Tedam is the lead for Social Work Practice Quality at Anglia Ruskin University where she has worked since 2016. Her research interests include human rights with a particular focus on children, cultural competency and legal frameworks for social work. She is also the past chair of the voluntary organisation AFRUCA (Africans Unite Against Child Abuse). Prospera is also a member of the Independent Families Returns Panel for the UK Border Agency.

Awura Adjoa is the pseudonym chosen by this author in order to maintain her anonymity. Originally from West Africa and now a university graduate, Awura sees it as her duty to share her experiences of a childhood which was disrupted as a result of being labelled a witch. She has a renewed commitment to making a difference in the lives of children who may be similarly affected or at risk of this form of abuse in the UK and abroad.

Foreword

By the early 1970s when I started working in child protection, health and welfare professionals were experiencing the shockwaves from the observations of luminaries such as Frederic Silverman and Henry Kempe who in 1962 published The Battered-Child Syndrome in the *Journal of the American Medical Association*. Many practitioners were incredulous that apparently caring parents could knowingly neglect and harm their children. Our imaginations were stretched further when, during the 1980s, the extent of child sexual abuse became apparent. I recall working with the mother of a ten-day-old baby, whose extensive internal damage was inflicted by her father, a convicted paedophile. I then watched attentively as a boy, whose body was severely limited by cerebral palsy, resolutely tapped out on his word-board his experiences of sexual exploitation. Had I not directly witnessed the aftermath of such violations, I would have found them hard to believe. How could anyone sexually assault such very vulnerable children? We learned that the mantra for all of us working in the field of child development and welfare had to be: imagine the unimaginable; believe the unbelievable; think the unthinkable.

Witchcraft accusations might seem to be consigned to history. The Salem or Pendle witch trials were events of a long bygone age and any modern witchcraft, particularly involving children, is the stuff of fairytale or fantasy such as *Sleeping Beauty*, *Harry Potter* or *The Worst Witch*. Nevertheless, unimaginable as it is, children throughout the world, including those living in Britain and other largely secular societies, suffer from being denounced as witches. Consequently, as well as isolation and stigma, they may have to endure beatings and starvation and some are killed. And yet would a child labelled as a witch, if able to disclose this, be believed? Might teachers and other professionals simply assume that she has an over-active imagination or, if traumatised by other life experiences, that she is merely recounting nightmares with no foundation in reality? A similar inability to believe children was common in the early days of our 'discovery' of the extent and nature of sexual abuse. The only way of ensuring vulnerable children are protected is to become fully informed of the relevant dynamics and to view the abuse from the victims' perspective.

This pioneering book provides essential information and insights. Awura Adjoa does not have to stretch her imagination because she directly experienced being denounced as a witch while living in Britain. In the early chapters her childhood experiences are recounted, along with analyses and prompts designed to explore readers' thoughts and emotions engendered by the narrative. The later chapters apply theory to the issues and explore frameworks for assessing and responding to the labelling of children as witches. Additionally, the book provides insights into wider social issues around migration, culture, beliefs and family dynamics.

When faced with the potentially unimaginable, unbelievable and unthinkable, we need those who understand the issues, like Awura Adjoa and Prospera Tedam, to guide our thoughts so that we can appreciate the dynamics and recognise what is happening. I have great pleasure in recommending this groundbreaking book to all those who work in the field of childcare and who are committed to the principles of anti-discriminatory practice and are motivated to ensure that, whatever their background and culture, children are appropriately understood and protected.

Celia Doyle (PhD)
Safeguarding Children Consultant

Acknowledgements

We would like to acknowledge the support and encouragement of a number of people over the course of writing this book. We would like to thank our families, friends and colleagues for their faith in our abilities. We also wish to acknowledge Critical Publishing for seeing the potential of this book and for their unflinching support towards making this a reality.

Also, Harry Venning (*Clare in the Community*), who provided the visuals to bring Awura Adjoa's narrative to life.

To Dr Celia Doyle, a supportive mentor and friend who has continued to encourage me over the years, urging me to continue to develop my writing through publication.

Above all, 'Awura Adjoa', whose tenacity, strength and resilience has resulted in this book and while we are joint authors, it would not have been possible to produce this book without her narrative.

Introduction

WHY A BOOK ON WITCHCRAFT LABELLING?

It has been suggested that in the past, social work has contributed to the marginalisation of minority voices in practice and research. However, the profession's growing concern with social justice, human rights, equality and fairness has resulted in an increase in knowledge creation by and with members of various minority groups (Figueira-McDonough et al, 2001).

By its very nature, this subject of witchcraft-related abuse is not one that can be researched and written about with ease due to its complex, sensitive and contentious content. It can be considered a 'hidden' crime, because while we may have a sense that witchcraft labelling is occurring, there is little empirical evidence except when its impact has been fatal and has become a subject of national enquiry (Victoria Climbié, Kristy Bamu, Khyra Ishaq), for example. The majority of existing literature approaches witchcraft labelling from a theoretical perspective, describing what it is, where and how it occurs, the possible outcomes for its victims and practitioner intervention – see Tedam (2014, 2016).

Other social work researchers who have written about witchcraft and spirit possession have done so within the context of broader child safeguarding literature (see for example Davies and Duckett, 2016) or within the context of religion and belief (Furness and Gilligan, 2010) or within the context of safeguarding black children (Tedam, 2016).

Non-governmental organisations such as Africans Unite against Child Abuse (AFRUCA) and the Victoria Climbié Foundation (VCF) have been proactive in raising awareness of this form of abuse in the UK and elsewhere and have engaged in community education and supporting parents.

AFRUCA, for example, has produced a range of accessible brochures and leaflets explaining this form of abuse and recommending parenting strategies which are consistent with child safeguarding principles. In addition, they provide training to practitioners on this form of abuse and continue to deliver services on behalf of local authority childcare teams, courts and schools.

The VCF, a charity set up after the murder and enquiry into the death of Victoria Climbié, also provides community awareness raising, particularly to faith groups and churches (Dioum and Yorath, 2013).

Researchers like Furness and Gilligan (2010) address the topic within a broader context of religion and belief and examine the significance of these in the lives of service users. The importance of social workers becoming more confident and competent when working with families whose faith is an important variable in their lives is also examined. Briggs et al (2011) reported on an evaluation which examined witchcraft and spirit possession among African communities in London and reached a number of key findings: 1) Where a belief in spirit possession existed, the abuse of children could be categorised under existing forms of abuse (physical, emotional, neglect and sexual). Consequently, existing child protection frameworks were found to be useful. 2) The belief in witchcraft and spirit possession was more widespread than the abuse associated with it. 3) Knowledge of culture and faith and the ability to work in a culturally sensitive and competent manner is critical to non-oppressive social work practice.

Issues of witchcraft and spirit possession have been reported in other professions and disciplines such as in school nursing (Obadina, 2012), mental health (Adewuya and Oguntade, 2007) and medicine (Hjelm and Mufunda, 2010).

Despite what appears to be a growth in research and literature in this area, there are still 'gaps' which we felt we could address through this book because:

1.   We provide a first-hand narrative from an adult who experienced witchcraft labelling during her childhood.

2.   The narrative gives insight into what appeared to be an 'ordinary' family doing 'ordinary' things.

3.   The analyses is provided by a qualified social work academic, registered with the HCPC, who takes the reader through theoretical and practice concepts as well as providing opportunities for reflection.

4.   The book will be a useful addition to resources used by a range of child welfare practitioners, parents, policy makers and faith leaders, and could be adapted for younger audiences where appropriate.

5.   The book has undergone peer review and scrutiny and could be a reference book for students and researchers who may be interested in this area of practice.

The authors have chosen this time and space to sensitively, carefully and accurately outline the childhood experiences of Awura Adjoa while analysing her experiences using a safeguarding children frame of reference.

Every effort has been made to ensure that the analyses, reflective questions and links to theoretical and practice-based models are clear, relevant and applicable to contemporary social work practice. Other professionals who work in the area of child protection and safeguarding may also find this a valuable resource.

The main aim of this book is to reiterate the ever-changing nature of abuse and to emphasise the danger created by the ongoing silence within some ethnic minority communities about practices and beliefs which can have detrimental consequences for children and which have previously resulted in serious case reviews, specifically in England.

The build-up of resentment towards Awura Adjoa and the escalation of punitive behaviours, attitudes and practices towards her were not picked up at the time. With the benefit of hindsight, we recognise how easy it would have been for any professional to have missed the signs, especially as Awura Adjoa herself appeared to be very good at concealing her emotions and trauma due to fear of reprisal from her family and community.

We have chosen to share this narrative in the way we have because we recognise the importance of constructing knowledge through this experience and we want to make available to childcare practitioners, policy makers, researchers and students a lived experience from which learning can be achieved and knowledge gained.

In addition, the authors want to draw the readers into the world of the child while at the same time addressing professional and practice issues and dilemmas.

Coulshed and Orme (2006) propose that social workers should continuously ask the *why* question of their service users in order to better understand situations and to inform their practice. Munro and Hubbard (2011) suggest that social workers should use their investigative skills and expertise to facilitate information sharing.

An unintended yet relevant outcome of this book has been the opportunity to provide a deeper and more robust conceptualisation of wider social issues around migration, culture, parenting practices, faith and beliefs, as well as family dynamics.

This is an ambitious yet hopeful book as it is one of the first of its kind to address the dearth of literature on this very important subject.

MEDIA REPORTING OF WITCHCRAFT LABELLING

Shocking rise in ritual child abuse cases linked to WITCHCRAFT reported to police

Boy, 15, 'tortured to death with hammer and chisels on Christmas Day because relative thought he was a witch'

RITUAL CHILD ABUSE LINKED TO WITCHCRAFT ON
THE RISE IN THE UK: DROWNING AND RAPE PART
OF 'HIDDEN CRIMES TO DRIVE OUT THE DEVIL'

- Metropolitan Police have 27 reports of witchcraft-based child abuse this year.

- In 2004, just two instances of faith-based abuse were reported to detectives.

- Cases include children being dunked in bath or beaten by church pastors.

- Relatives believe the children have been totally possessed by evil spirits.

- A new DVD shows teachers and youth workers how to spot signs of abuse.

- DVD debut today at London debate on growing problem of ritual child abuse.

- Met's Det Supt Terry Sharpe: 'Regardless of the beliefs, abuse is abuse'.

- Victoria Climbié, eight, and Kristy Bamu, 15, both died after ritual abuse.

(MailOnline, October 2014)

ORGANISATION OF THE BOOK

This book is unique in that its content is largely the narrative of Awura Adjoa, a young West African girl who joined her parents in the UK after living apart from them for the first ten years of her life. Awura Adjoa tells the story as it is, initially identifying what appears to be a fairly standard way of life to highlighting practices and behaviours which could or should have been challenged. Tedam interjects throughout this narrative, offering a contemporary evidence-informed perspective of what may have been happening while also integrating social science theory, relevant legislation and policy, some practice dilemmas and reflections which will be useful for childcare professionals generally and social work practitioners more specifically.

The book is purposely structured to enable readers to decide how they wish to engage with its contents. Some may choose to approach it one chapter at a time, in which case each chapter can be a standalone read, or alternatively readers can digest larger portions at a time to gain a broader understanding of the key issues raised.

This book is divided into Parts 1 and 2, consisting of ten chapters which take the reader through the life course of Awura Adjoa, a child victim of witchcraft labelling. The chapter headings represent the journey through which Awura Adjoa travelled. Her narratives are interspersed with reflective questions, learning points and discussions which will be of importance to social workers, education and health professionals, as well as any researchers, policy makers and students interested in understanding this form of child abuse. This book will also be useful to parents who may be at risk of parenting in this way and require 'evidence' to show that this is unacceptable and unwarranted in the life of a child. It gives significant others a process through which they might report such actions.

Part 1 (Chapters 1–7) Narrative and analyses

Chapter 1 introduces the reader to the beginning of the narrative which starts in West Africa as Awura Adjoa prepares to leave the continent.

In Chapter 2, we join Awura Adjoa on her journey to the United Kingdom and catch a glimpse into her innermost hopes for her 'new life'. Awura Adjoa is reunited with her parents and her siblings and begins to settle into her new host country

In Chapter 3, we begin to see how Awura Adjoa's hopes for a better life in the new country are gradually fading as misunderstandings start to emerge, leaving her vulnerable and unhappy.

The narrative in Chapter 4 continues pretty much along the lines of the previous chapter. Awura Adjoa has been labelled a *witch* and becomes tainted, ostracised and isolated.

Chapter 5, titled 'Confess you must', presents the reader with some difficult experiences and practices, highlighting attempts by Awura Adjoa's parents to secure a 'confession' from her about being a witch.

In Chapter 6, Awura Adjoa is returned to West Africa following a period of maltreatment and exclusion.

Chapter 7 finds Awura Adjoa in West Africa with relatives and her narrative concludes with some reflection on where she is now.

Part 2 (Chapters 8–10) Implications for practice

Chapters 8, 9 and 10 provide more of a discussion about theory and practice issues linked directly to Awura Adjoa's narrative.

Chapter 8 specifically highlights a few relevant theories such as attachment, stigma, labelling, gender, human growth and development, Maslow's hierarchy of needs and family systems theories. The discussion in this chapter also makes links to the Professional Capabilities Framework (PCF) and HCPC standards of proficiency, knowledge and skills statement for child and family social workers, as well as values and ethics.

A practice dilemma discussion follows, addressing the complexities and challenges that might be faced by social workers who may hold similar beliefs and views about witchcraft.

Chapter 9 examines some frameworks for recognising and responding to witchcraft labelling. Some ideas for teaching and learning in the area of witchcraft labelling are proposed, as well as assessment and engagement frameworks.

Chapter 10 is the final chapter, which attempts to bring together the main ideas and arguments presented in the book and also offers recommendations for practice.

In addition to the ten main chapters, the book has the following features throughout:

Reflective questions

Analyses

Chapter summaries

Feelings and learning check

Further reading

TERMINOLOGY AND KEY CONCEPTS

In this section, we offer a brief discussion of the key terminology used within this book to aid readers' understanding as they engage with the contents of this book. We acknowledge the range of definitions and the absence of a universally agreed definition for many of these terms. The value and importance of a common understanding from the outset cannot be overemphasised.

According to Goddard (2012), the term *spirit possession* or *witchcraft* is known by many other names in different parts of Africa, notably:

- *Abazimu* (Rwanda);
- *Aje* (Yorubaland, Nigeria);
- *Emandwa* (Uganda);
- *Ndoki* or *Kindoki* (Congo);
- *Djinn* or *evil eye* (Tanzania);
- *Ogbanje* or *Amozu* (Igboland, Nigeria).

Categories of abuse

Sexual abuse

The Department for Education (2015, p 38) defines sexual abuse as '*forcing or enticing a child or young person to take part in sexual activities*'. Sexual activities are defined as:

penetration… or non-penetrative acts such as masturbation, kissing, rubbing and touching outside of clothing… involving children in looking at, or in the production of sexual images, watching sexual activities, encouraging children to behave in sexually inappropriate ways or grooming a child in preparation for abuse.

(DfE, 2015, p 38)

Physical abuse

'*Hitting, shaking, throwing, poisoning, burning or scalding, drowning, suffocating or otherwise causing physical harm to a child*' (DfE, 2015, p 92).

Emotional abuse

the persistent emotional maltreatment of a child such as to cause severe and persistent adverse effects on the child's emotional development. It may involve conveying to a child that they are worthless or unloved, inadequate, or valued only insofar as they meet the needs of another person. It may include not giving the child opportunities to express their views, deliberately silencing them or making fun of what they say or communicate… It may involve seeing or hearing the ill-treatment of another. It may involve serious bullying (including cyber-bullying) causing children frequently to feel frightened or in danger, or the exploration or corruption of children.

(Department of Health 2010, p 38)

Fasting is the purposeful withholding and abstaining from food and water for a specific period of time for medical, religious or other reasons. Fasting is practiced in Islam and also in various Christian denominations.

INTRODUCTION

If our lives weren't constantly told and retold, storying each new experience, we would have no coherent notion of who we are, where we are going, what we believe, what we want, where we belong and how to be.

(Bolton, 2006, p 206)

It has been the case that child cruelty, maltreatment and abuse can be difficult to prevent, primarily because it relies largely on self-reporting or the proactive responses by professionals who come into contact with children and young people on a regular basis. These proactive responses rely on professionals being able to not only read and interpret signs and signals but also to have an understanding of a wide range of socio-cultural factors affecting individuals, families and communities in the UK.

Child abuse linked to accusations of witchcraft and spirit possession is a growing phenomenon in the UK and globally (Bottoms et al, 1995; Goddard, 2012); however, it has largely been underestimated and trivialised. It is not a new phenomenon (Wolfgang, 2004); however, growing awareness of broader child safeguarding concepts is resulting in many families, groups and communities talking about and exposing its causes and harmful effects while offering potential strategies to minimise its prevalence.

Historically, the belief in witchcraft existed across the world and Acts of Parliament in Europe prosecuted people who were accused of being witches, such as through the Witchcraft Act 1735 in England.

Witchcraft has a long history, from the medieval era until the present day and has also been viewed as a positive skill. While the Lancaster witchcraft trials resulted from a negative view of witchcraft, research suggests that there are also 'good' witches (Wolfgang, 2004).

The *Salem witch trials* which were carried out in Massachusetts, British North America (1692–1693), illustrates how widespread the belief in witchcraft was throughout the British colonies. There was also the view that witches were older females (Douglas, 1970).

Pearson (2010) has suggested that historically, 85 per cent of those accused of witchcraft have been female, and Douglas (1970) adds that these used to be older females.

More recently in the UK, the deaths of Victoria Climbié and Kristy Bamu as well as the torso found in the River Thames (Adam) represent tragedies in which children were believed to have been connected to witchcraft in some way or the other. The circumstances which resulted in the death of these children will be explored later in the book.

It is important therefore to clarify from the outset that the construct of *witchcraft* used here denotes an African perspective which largely views witchcraft as negative, evil and destructive (AFRUCA, 2009).

According to the Department for Education and Skills (2007) a *witch* is defined as a person possessed with evil power to harm others while *spirit possession* is the belief that an evil force has entered a person in order to control and direct their harm towards others to harm others.

Hermkens (2015) has also argued that witchcraft accusations have much to do with gender and power and these two factors, which will be discussed in much more depth, are present in this narrative.

In 2006, Stobart undertook a systematic review of child abuse cases in the UK, which involved 47 children from Africa, Europe and South Asia where there was some link to witchcraft accusations, and found that 20 of these cases involved children from 'Christian' homes. Stobart also found that five of the children were physically abused in their places of worship. It is not the aim of this book to single out or label any one faith or religion for scrutiny; however, it must be continually acknowledged that Awura Adjoa's narrative, which is the focus of this book, involves a Christian Pentecostal church, its associated beliefs and the faith which the church subscribed to. We are certain that the majority of churches and faith groups are well-meaning; however, this does not detract from nor minimise Awura Adjoa's experiences contained herein. It is also critical to note that Briggs et al (2011) found that 64 per cent of Africans described themselves as Christian.

In addition, Stobart (2006) identified the following West African countries as having the highest prevalence of witchcraft-related abuse: Benin, Cameroon, Ghana and Nigeria. This view is corroborated by Adinkrah (2011) who suggests, for example, that 90 per cent of Ghanaian people believe in witchcraft. This finding is significant because Awura Adjoa is from a country in West Africa.

There are many examples where deep-seated beliefs and confidence in a message delivered or propagated by a pastor/motivational speaker or some other person held in high esteem has resulted in the abuse and death of children globally. A case in point is the book *To Train Up A Child*, which was supposed to offer parents strategies to manage their children's behaviour, written by Michael and Debi Pearl (Pearl and Pearl, 2009), who led what has been described as an evangelical church (Joyce, 2013).

There are *three* reported cases of fatal child cruelty in the United States which have been directly linked to the contents of the book and its authors.

The first child was four-year-old Sean Paddock who died in 2006 after his mother suffocated him using blankets as a form of discipline (Felker, 2007).

In 2010, Lydia Schatz died after reports that she had been beaten, three years after arriving in California from Liberia. The third case is one which we will discuss in some depth due to what we perceive as bearing striking similarities to the experiences of Awura Adjoa.

Hana and her brother Immanuel were adopted from Ethiopia and brought to the United States. Their adoptive parents, Carri and Larry Williams, described as *devout fundamentalist Christians*, believed in the teachings of their pastor and purchased his book. They claim to have followed the guidance and instructions presented in the book and ended up with a dead child, Hana aged 13. It has been reported that they hit and starved their daughter and also gave her frozen food and often left her outside in the winter as a form of punishment. The paediatrician who examined the child said she died of malnutrition and hypothermia, and concluded that the book (*To Train Up a Child*) could easily be misinterpreted and result in significant abuse of children.

All parents were subsequently convicted for unlawful capital punishment and manslaughter (BBC, 2013).

During the trial of Carri and Larry Williams, the court heard that Hana's experiences had been characterised by regular abusive disciplinary methods which intensified as time went on. Some of her experiences included:

- being forced to sleep alone in a barn outside the main family house;
- being locked away in a 4x2 ft closet;
- made to use an outdoor portable toilet (cleaned a couple of times a year by her mother);
- made to have her showers in the front yard under a hose with no privacy;
- being served different meals from the biological children, usually cold or frozen food, regardless of the weather or time of year;
- not being allowed to take part in family celebrations like birthdays and Christmas;
- could go for days without being spoken to by her parents or siblings;
- being beaten with a range of instruments, including a plastic tube and a belt;
- being home schooled and punished for getting work wrong.

The story about Hana is deeply distressing for a number of reasons and more so because she was adopted from what appeared to have been an orphanage in Ethiopia. Her brother Immanuel had a hearing impairment, and although he experienced maltreatment and abuse, did not suffer the same fate as his sister Hana. He subsequently went into a foster placement with a diagnosis of post-traumatic stress disorder.

▶▶   ***FURTHER READING***

Joyce, K (2013) Hana's story: An adoptee's tragic fate, and how it could happen again. [online] Available at: www.slate.com/articles/ double_x/doublex/2013/11/hana_williams_the_tragic_death_ of_an_ethiopian_adoptee_and_how_it_could.html (accessed 18 March 2017).

REFLECTIVE QUESTION

What have you learned from the stories of these three American children?

Research suggests that the belief in witchcraft and spirit possession exists across faiths, cultures and countries and should not be viewed as a problem for a specific faith, culture or community. For example, Khyra Ishaq, a Muslim child from Birmingham who was also dual heritage (white British and black African-Caribbean), was considered to be possessed by *Jinn*, which in some Islamic practices refers to a belief in spirit possession. For all intents and purposes, Khyra was a vulnerable child. In particular, she was home-tutored, which meant that she had little contact with teachers and other education professionals who may have been able to intervene and prevent the fatality that eventually occurred. The word *jinn* is derived from the Arabic *ijtinan*, which means '*to be concealed from sight*' (Sheikh, 2005, p 339).

There is also the case of Tunde, an eight-year-old female child of Angolan heritage, who was severely '*beaten with a belt buckle and stabbed with a stiletto shoe*' had '*chilli pepper rubbed in her eyes*' and was '*sliced with a kitchen knife*'. These were believed to be acts of exorcism inflicted by adult members of her family who believed she had '*kindoki*' (Keeble and Hollington, 2011, pp 116–17).

Exorcisms, also sometimes referred to as *deliverance*, were:

performed on people and things, both in imprecatory and deprecatory forms. As imprecations, the exorcisms directly adjured Satan or the demons to leave the candidate (or object); as deprecations they implored God to release the persons or objects from demonic power. These spoken formulas were usually accompanied by some kind of action or gesture (hand-laying, blowing upon or hissing/spitting at the candidate/demon) and posture or position (kneeling upon goatskin, arms stretched out.

(Linards, 2011, p 2)

Throughout this book, the authors have avoided the use of the term *branding* and have chosen instead to use *labelling*. While this could be viewed as a matter of semantics, the authors perceive the use of the word *branding* to not adequately capture the sentiment being projected in this book. Prospera Tedam's own previous work (Tedam, 2014) used the word *branding*. Sociologically, *labelling* appears to be better linked to the area under discussion and also more appropriate for the audience for whom the book is intended. Furthermore, *labelling theory* attempts to explain how specific labels often result in people behaving in ways that are consistent with the label. Awura Adjoa tells us that she felt '*evil*' and '*kept away from other children for fear of contaminating them*'.

Also, the use of the term *safeguarding* rather than *child protection* is used throughout this book and again is consistent with the policy shift from a reactive to a preventative approach. According to the Department for Education (2006), safeguarding is:

The process of protecting children from abuse or neglect, preventing impairment of their health and development, and ensuring they are growing up in circumstances consistent with the provision of safe and effective care that enables children to have optimum life chances and enter adulthood successfully.

(DfE, 2006, p 5)

METHODOLOGY

Narrative inquiry, the methodological approach used for this book, is a co-production by the expert by experience and the researcher/academic. This method ensures dignity, well-being and privacy in the way in which the narrative is written, analysed and presented. According to Clandinin (2007), the narrative researcher plays two roles – one is being in a close relationship with the participant and the other is having a professional responsibility to the community of scholars.

This book is more than '*collaboration between researcher and participants*' (Clandinin and Connelly, 2000, p 20) but rather is an in-depth case study which Awura Adjoa controls in terms of what and how she writes. Her narrative is presented in its original form, written by Awura Adjoa herself, a previous child victim of witchcraft labelling. As the academic involved, Tedam offers some analyses of her experiences, grounding it in contemporary theoretical and philosophical understandings while providing a view on the ways in which social workers and other childcare practitioners might work with Awura Adjoa and her family if this were to occur in the present day.

It could also be suggested that this methodology mirrors case-study research, which according to Yin (2010) focuses on an in-depth consideration of one or a few stories or (cases). Remenyi (2012) suggests that case studies need to have a storyline which can be followed and understood. The narrative presented follows a logical and coherent storyline.

Additionally, Schulkind et al (2012) suggest that women show greater fluency in retrieving autobiographical memories in comparison with men and that their autobiographical narratives are more detailed, more coherent, more emotional and longer than those produced by men. They further state that women are more likely to mention the thoughts and feelings of others in their narratives. Awura Adjoa does this exceptionally well in her vivid descriptions, which also meant that two significant events were captured visually through illustrations.

The knowledge gained from undertaking this work continues to highlight the centrality of service user experiences, particularly in relation to sensitive issues which have been minimally researched and explored.

In social work, there has been a growing recognition of the value of co-production in research to inform service delivery, yet there is variation as to how this is understood (Cummins and Miller, 2007).

The underlying principles of collaborative working, fairness, respect for the views of others and shared learning underpin this publication. Here we explain our perspectives and motivation for producing this book.

Prospera Tedam's account

Awura Adjoa made contact with me and described some of her experiences, following the publication of a theoretical paper (Tedam, 2014) in which I concluded that more empirical research involving people who had experienced witchcraft labelling was required. She wanted to know whether her story would make a difference to the general public and protect other children who may be at risk of similar harm. Following a period of discussion and consultation, we came up with the idea of this book and further thought was given as to how we might approach the task to make it meaningful for social work and other childcare professionals. My identity as a black African female and my familiarity with the concept of *witchcraft* meant that I felt able to contribute to the development of this book. In the spirit of co-production, Awura Adjoa wrote her own narrative. We did not follow the 'conventional' process of interview, transcribing, member checking etc as there was an agreement that the process, learning and journey would be a shared one and in line with our individual areas of expertise – Awura Adjoa as the expert of her experience would contribute her narrative and I would attempt a critical appraisal, drawing upon research, ideas and concepts which would speak to various childcare professionals and social workers specifically. We also considered that this book would be a valuable resource for faith leaders, congregants, policy makers, educators, parents and young people; consequently, we had to carefully consider the audience during our writing. Awura Adjoa does not consider herself a service user nor a victim. She has focused on telling her story in a factual, chronological manner and has been honest enough to explain that she has chosen to omit specific experiences which could easily identify her and/or her family.

Awura Adjoa's account

I really want people to understand that being labelled a witch is very common in some societies and cultures and the fact that people live in the UK or outside their home countries does not make much of a difference to many. I was an ordinary girl coming to join my ordinary parents – who could have suspected that I would face the treatment that I did? For all the families out there looking to scapegoat their children and young relatives, by labelling them as witches, think again!

WHAT IS WITCHCRAFT?

Stobart (2006) suggests that there is no universally accepted definition or consensus on what witchcraft is; nonetheless, it is widely understood to be linked to the entry of evil spirits into a person, causing them to become evil and capable of harm, destruction and misfortune (Bartholomew, 2015).

It has been suggested by AFRUCA (2009, p 7) that witchcraft is based on the belief in 'the existence of a dark world inhabited by innate beings who are in constant interaction with the living in the physical world where humans live' and that they have the 'power to override human wills and wishes' and 'manifest their powers through human agents'.

This definition is packed with many interesting concepts and ideas which are worthy of further analysis. The mention of witchcraft being manifest through human agents is significant to Awura Adjoa's narrative and will be examined in greater detail later.

Another term that is frequently used is faith-based abuse. According to AFRUCA (2014), the term faith-based abuse can be used to describe a range of abuse including ritualistic abuse (human sacrifice or sexual acts), exorcism rites that cause emotional and physical harm, and withholding of medical treatment in favour of prayer. The term clergy abuse has also been used to refer to abuse by, for example, the clergy within the Catholic Church (Kline et al, 2008), and the significance of this definition within this book stems from the attachment and connection to church leaders, a theme which we will revisit later on.

Canda and Furman (2009) suggest that there is a strong link between ethnicity, race and religious affiliations and Twum-Danso Imoh (2012) identifies the influence of Christianity on the physical punishment of children in countries such as Ghana.

Gershman (2015) states that witchcraft beliefs are heterogeneous because people express these variably, in different countries and within different communities. He argues that the gender, age and backgrounds of people believed to possess witchcraft varies significantly. For example, it has been suggested that in South Africa, AIDS was blamed on witchcraft (Niehaus, 2013), as was the Ebola epidemic in Sierra Leone (Tedam, 2016).

It is important to acknowledge that there is a body of research examining a different type of Witchcraft, which is described as relating to 'Pagan spirituality' (Yardley, 2008, p 329), and which is differentiated from other definitions of witchcraft by the use of a capital 'W'. We wish to restate that this is not the construct of witchcraft used in this book.

As authors, we felt able to produce our own definition of witchcraft labelling towards the end of the book, drawing upon all of the key concepts taken from Awura Adjoa's narrative. We hope this will be a useful contribution to what we believe to be a complex area of contemporary social work practice.

Who can be labelled?

Contrary to some views that this form of abuse is 'cultural' and occurs in ethnic minority families and within their communities, there is evidence to suggest that accusations of witchcraft and spirit possession exist among some populations in Papua New Guinea (Hermkens, 2015), in parts of rural India (Chaudhury, 2012) and of course historically in the UK (La Fontaine, 2009) and the United States (Mercer, 2012).

In addition, research suggests that this form of abuse is not specific to any one faith or religious ideology. There is also evidence of it in Islam (Sheik, 2005) and Traditional African Religion (Adinkrah, 2004).

Finally, witchcraft-related abuse and accusations of spirit possession are gender neutral, and children and vulnerable adults from either gender can be labelled. That said, research suggests that in some countries accusations are biased towards women (Adinkrah, 2004).

It would appear that historically '*many Africans took what they wanted from Christianity and blended it with their own traditions*' (Cavendish, 1994, p 101) and there are many parts of the Bible which some Christians have used to 'justify' the abuse meted out to people who have been labelled. It is not within the scope of this book to fully examine Christianity, Christian beliefs or scriptures contained within the Bible, as these issues are not only contentious but could also give rise to cautiousness by parents and families when discussing issues relating to their faith. It is expedient to give some examples of biblical verses that have been used to justify abuse and harm towards children.

> Proverbs 13:24: '*He that spareth his rod, hateth his son: but he that loveth him chastneth him.*'
> Proverbs 23:13: '*Withhold not correction from the child: for if thou beatest him with the rod, he shall not die.*'
> Proverbs 23:14: '*Thou shalt beat him with the rod, and shalt deliver his soul from hell (Shoel).*'
>
> (The King James Version (KJV) of the Bible)

Beliefs affecting behaviour

There is a growing body of knowledge about the ways in which personal, family and community beliefs can affect our behaviours and attitudes. The overarching consideration here is not about *what* we believe, but rather *how* our beliefs make us act. **Fact** – everyone has beliefs. Some of our beliefs are deeply rooted in our upbringing, through our interactions with others or through our churches, communities and societies. Beliefs can change over time, increasing or decreasing in intensity as we mature and grow in awareness and take into account research evidence and advancements in science and technology.

According to Stabell (2010), various societies explain misfortune in different ways. He suggests that people from the West use the biomedical model to explain illness and that people of South Asian origin are more likely to blame misfortune using a moral causal ontological position (bad karma). This makes it all the more necessary for social workers to understand the ways in which their clients and/or service users explain ill luck and unfortunate situations.

This is similar to Gilligan's view (2009), which states that a person's beliefs inform and influence the way in which they view the world and make decisions.

At this juncture, we would like to introduce readers to Awura Adjoa's narrative.

Part 1 Narrative and analyses

1   In the beginning

In the beginning… always a good place to start isn't it? From the very beginning. I would describe my feelings then as excited, nervous but also full of joy because I was about to experience a new life. In the beginning, life as I knew it as a girl consisted of getting up for school and coming back home. At home, I would help with the chores and then of course in the evening, I would sit near the feet of the older women listening to stories about the history of my country and the rich culture. This was the daily living which I enjoyed and had become accustomed to. It was these little things that made growing up in this part of West Africa even more interesting. Different stories were told each evening and I always looked forward to this part of the day.

My journey to the Western part of the world began when my parents decided it was time for me to come and join them in the United Kingdom. They had been in the UK for ten years and I had lived apart from them all this while. I was the third of five children and both of my parents were educated. West Africa was the only place I had been exposed to and the joy that filled me at the thought of leaving is still indescribable. I did not grow up with my parents; I had lived with different relatives and so for me the best part of this decision was that I was going to have the chance to finally live with and be brought up by my parents. I remember going to school and not knowing whether to tell my friends or not about my planned relocation to the United Kingdom. Of course in the African culture, particularly from a West African point of view, a person was not allowed to reveal their plans until the point had arrived for the plan to be executed. So for me, as a child, it was the longest-kept secret and each day I would go to school, be excited but could not share my excitement with anyone. I would go through the weekend with prayer and fasting, which I was told was necessary, hoping that my application for a visa would be successful.

REFLECTIVE QUESTION

How would you address a situation in which a ten-year-old child disclosed that they were required by their parent/carer to engage in a period of fasting (abstaining from food and drink)?

Day in, day out, I waited, expecting and looking forward to seeing my uncle who had been entrusted to take me through the visa application process while I was in West Africa. The experience began with taking pictures, practising for interviews as I was very shy and waiting on phone calls from immigration solicitors. Then one day, one early afternoon, my uncle came and collected me from school and we went to the British High Commission in my town. There were many people as I queued up, just a little girl, unaware of the struggles other people had to go through to acquire a visa for the United Kingdom. With the slow movement of the queue, we made our way through what seemed to be a well-coordinated system and we were given a number and waited for it to be called out. Finally I heard my number being called out. I remember my uncle was not allowed to come in with me; I was very scared, I did not know what to expect. I was only ten years old and as I approached what seemed to be a counter I could feel my legs shaking. However, the lady who was sitting at the other end of the glass screen was so nice that it made the whole process so much easier for me. I remember her asking me to put my fingers on something that looked like a camera but just for fingers. She took me through the whole screening process and asked me a couple of questions. I told her how excited I was because I was going to get to see my parents; she told me, 'I'm excited for you' when she was done with the interview.

REFLECTIVE QUESTION

What are your views about Awura Adjoa, a ten-year-old child, being on her own during the interview for a visa at the British High Commission?

I came out of the room, looked out at the crowd in the waiting area and I saw that my uncle's hands were high up in the air so that I could see him waiting for me from within the crowd. He had the biggest smile on his face and he asked me how it went. I told him how scared I had felt and he held me as tight as he could to reassure me that everything was fine. I told him about the woman at the counter and how she said she was happy for me. We laughed and bought some food as we made our way back home. Barely a week later my uncle came back and picked me up from home and we went back to that same British High Commission with long queues of people. I remember wondering why people woke up that early to go there, only to be in a queue for so long. I thought to myself, 'What was the purpose, surely it is as simple as applying for something and waiting for a reply?', but of course this was not always the case for some people.

That fateful day my queueing up was for a very different reason. My uncle explained to me that following my conversation with the nice woman the week before, a decision had been made about whether I would be given permission to join my parents and I was here to find out what that decision was. I followed my uncle in the queue into the waiting area. I watched him sit nervously, with his fists clenched and legs shaking. Finally, my name was called out and he stood up and looked down at me, reached out to take my hand; I took it, got up and followed him to the counter where an envelope was handed over to us. I was smiling because for me I thought surely this is the best news ever and that whatever was needed to facilitate my going to see my parents was in that envelope.

We came out of the waiting area, continued out of the actual building and then made our way outside where hundreds of other people lined up. My uncle looked at me and then he said, 'Should we?' I replied in our local dialect and said, 'Should we what?' He then said, 'Should we open it and see what they have concluded?' I remember feeling so nervous but then I looked at his face and he looked even more anxious than I did. Slowly he ripped open that first part of the envelope, took out my passport and opened it. He suddenly jumped up and screamed a loud 'YES' and then said, 'You got it!' I remember being so happy and shouting and screaming 'Yes, yes, yes, yes, yes!' and then in my local dialect I said, 'I am going abroad; I am going to the land where things will be better than how it has been so far'. A decision had been made, a decision that was going to take me to a foreign land; a decision that would take me closer to my parents. It couldn't get any better than this! I was over the moon!

In the few weeks that followed I became more and more excited. There was more joy, more happiness and a sense of urgency to leave the country. I couldn't wait. I went to school but still had to keep the secret. I went to church and I still had to keep the secret. My uncle had warned me to not tell anybody. He said to me that people wouldn't be as happy for me as I thought they ought to and that some people were envious. He impressed upon me that some people would try to ruin it for me and so it was best to keep it a secret for as long as possible until the last hour, I recall him saying.

My final weeks at school were some of the saddest days of my life. I was going to say goodbye to some of the best people I had known and spent my days with, teachers who had not only taught me but had also parented me while at school. Then one afternoon in that final week of school while I was in the classroom, I saw my uncle turn up as I looked out of the window, and I thought surely something was wrong. I wondered if I'd forgotten to do the house chores. I thought he was here to make a complaint about me. While I waited to find out what was happening, the headmistress called me to come up from the class-room into her office. As I got into the office I saw my classteacher standing with my uncle, both beaming with smiles, then my headmistress behind me said, 'Congratulations Awura Adjoa, we have heard the good news and we are really going to miss you but we know you are destined for great things and this is a new beginning for you'. It was then I understood why my uncle had come here. He had come here to share the best news ever and now my teachers and headmistress knew that I was going away. The news that I was going abroad for a better life soon reached many more teachers during the day. And that was it; my uncle had come to inform them and then to pick me up. It was three days before my journey and so to him that was leaving information until the last minute, like he had talked about.

My uncle picked me up and our first stop was to the market to purchase a few items of essential clothing which he felt I would need. I never really understood why I needed these clothes, after all, I was going to see my parents, right? There was no need to worry; nothing could go wrong. My parents were my parents. We went home and the three days could not come any sooner. Finally on the day of my planned travel, my uncle described what my journey was going to be like. I was going to go with a family friend (Mrs K), who also lived in the United Kingdom. She had come for a holiday and was taking her own children back with her. I was dropped off at their house and it was clear that Mrs K's children were better informed and had more knowledge about England than I had. That evening, they ordered pizza for dinner and it was my first time having pizza. I was so fascinated by the food and then we had tomato juice, which I absolutely hated! And I don't think I've ever tried tomato juice since then. We finished packing and we made our way to the airport to catch our flight.

It was also my first time at the airport and so on getting to the airport I felt very scared. I saw many people pulling and carrying their suitcases. Some seemed excited while others not so much. I also observed the number of queues, which for a second made me think all over again about the queuing process at the British High Commission. I stood there with the other children waiting for Mrs K and my uncle who had gone and joined one of the queues. They returned to inform us that we were no longer travelling that evening. It turned out there was a mechanical fault with the plane and so we had to wait three days before we could travel and this meant going to Mrs K's house for another three days. Three days came sooner rather than later and on the third day we embarked on the journey to that foreign land. The plane that was taking me to where it all began.

 ## Analysis

This introductory chapter has provided a background and context to Awura Adjoa's travel and relocation to the UK. It also provides some context to her life in West Africa. The narrative suggests that Awura Adjoa had been looked after by extended family for the first ten years of her life and had become accustomed to a way of life which involved adults and no other children her age within her home. Awura Adjoa refers to older people telling stories as one of the ways in which some families and communities spent their evenings. The stories told are usually educational and are aimed at 'teaching' life skills and transmitting experiences from one generation to another. Awura Adjoa clearly enjoyed the storytelling and had started to associate that with leisure activity to fill her evenings.

Awura Adjoa's uncle believed that family plans should not be shared as these could be thwarted by people who disliked a family and who sought to cause chaos within a family. This belief is very much in line with the belief in witchcraft, the supernatural and evil spirits.

One can only imagine the type of pressure and responsibility placed on children who have been asked and coerced into keeping secrets. The plans for Awura Adjoa to join her parents would have been a helpful disclosure; however, she is commended for managing to keep her travel plans private, as sharing this with her friends may have had undesirable consequences from members of her family. Awura Adjoa was encouraged to fast, a practice for which guidance is available in the UK, specifically in the context of Ramadan and Muslim children where caution is recommended for children under the age of 12.

Awura Adjoa was eventually to travel in the company of a family friend and her three children. Even at this stage there was a sense of a lack of preparedness for the journey and relocation to a new country. Again it was clear that in terms of involving the children in decision-making or at the very least preparing them for the journey, the three children were better prepared than Awura Adjoa. This is a useful area for consideration when preparing children and young people for transitions and changes. Harper (2016) refers to transitions to mean the process of change that is experienced when children move settings and environments while having to re-establish themselves in a new and unfamiliar environment. While she acknowledges that people are very likely to have several moves during their lifetime, for children, these transitions can have detrimental effects if not handled sensitively and with utmost care.

Many children and young people are separated from their families for various reasons, and research by Nzira (2011) suggests that this is widespread among migrants in the UK and that there are advantages and limitations to such practices. Some migrants to the UK prefer to leave their children and other dependents in the home country to enable them to establish themselves and settle in before making the commitment to reunite with them. This view is corroborated by Bledsoe and Sow (2011) who suggest that West African parents, by and large, view leaving their children with relatives in different households as normal and beneficial to the child's development.

The Children Act 1989 and the United Nations Convention on the Rights of the Child (UNCRC) clearly support the bringing up of children within their own families wherever possible, yet we know that there are many children for whom separation from their parents occurs as a result of migration (Mazzucato et al, 2015).

FEELINGS AND LEARNING CHECK

Consider how the narrative contained in this chapter has made you feel.

Reflect on what you knew before and what you have learned from this chapter.

CHAPTER SUMMARY

This chapter has provided an introduction into the early life experiences of Awura Adjoa and her preparation towards leaving West Africa to join her parents in the UK. We are given insight into the process of applying for a visa as well as family preparations for her travel. She affords us the opportunity to understand the wider family beliefs around the existence of 'evil' and the importance of fasting and prayer as facilitating the process of a good outcome. We begin to understand how the separation from her parents has impacted on her and her joy upon realising she would be reuniting with her parents.

FURTHER READING

Bledsoe, C H and Sow, P (2011) Back to Africa: Second Chances for the Children of West African Immigrants. Journal of Marriage and Family, 73(4): 747–62.

Mazzucato, V, Cebotari, V, Veale, A, White, A, Grassi, M and Vivet, J (2015) International Parental Migration and the Psychological Wellbeing of children in Ghana and Nigeria. Social Science & Medicine, 132: 215–24.

2 A foreign land

The flight felt like the longest period of my life and I was super excited. It was my first time on a plane and throughout the duration of the flight, I was eager to stand up and walk around to see more of this fish-looking thing that we were seated in. We arrived at Heathrow Airport at exactly seven o'clock in the morning; it was very cold and that was my first shock! I wondered whether there was a freezer nearby because that was the only thing I knew to be as cold as what I felt that morning. Mrs K quickly wrapped me up in a cardigan and scarf which she had because I wasn't suitably dressed, as not only was I coming from a hot country but also my uncle had not prepared me, clothing wise, for such weather. I lined up in a different queue to that of Mrs K and her family and they couldn't come with me because they were British citizens and so they had to join a different queue as we went through Immigration and Customs procedures.

REFLECTIVE QUESTION

What are your views about Awura Adjoa being separated from the adult who was responsible for her as they went through Immigration and Customs processes?

As I went through the queue and over to the other side, my excitement grew. I was seeing people with different coloured skin, which was new to me. I used to describe myself as light in complexion but that day I saw the real definition of light skin complexion and it was fascinating. Gradually we made our way out of the airport, where Mrs K's husband was waiting to pick us up.

My first thought was, where were my parents? They were the ones I was looking forward to seeing first, not this uncle who I wasn't told would be coming to pick us up. I followed Mrs K and everyone else to the parking lot where there was a car waiting for us. I was exhausted and so although I wanted to look out of the window at all the beautiful scenes outside, I just could not keep my eyes open and I dozed off as I had been awake during the entire flight and was now very tired. On opening my eyes, we had arrived at Mrs K's house, and we got out of the car. Our luggage was taken upstairs. I was very quiet and I felt more nervous than I had felt throughout the journey. This was because I had not seen my parents and yet I knew they were the ones I was coming to be with. Recognising how nervous I was, Mrs K came in, hugged me and said, 'Don't worry, your parents will be coming to pick you up tomorrow; you will see them then'.

REFLECTIVE QUESTIONS

What are your views about the length of time it took for Awura Adjoa to be reunited with her parents?

What, if anything, could Mrs K have done to minimise Awura Adjoa's nervousness?

We went to bed and the next day very early in the morning I woke up to what I was later told was a full English breakfast. That morning I also tried grapes for the first time and I couldn't stop stuffing my mouth with them because they tasted nice. I was excited; I was going to get to see my parents. Mrs K got me ready after breakfast, I said my goodbyes which made me feel sad because these were the very people I had begun this journey with but there was a sense of understanding that I would see them again; after all, we had come together so there was no leaving without each other, at least in my head that's what I thought. There appeared to be some change in the plan because Mrs K asked me to get into her car and she drove us off. Shortly afterwards, we arrived in what seemed like the biggest house I had seen since I arrived in this foreign land. On the journey to my parents' house I was seeing things I had never seen before: shops, traffic lights which back home people never really obeyed and then suddenly this big drive-through or driveway as I learned it was called. As we pulled into the driveway I saw a man beaming with the biggest smile I had ever seen, looking at me. I got out of the car and I had something in my hand which I clinged onto even more, while staring at the man who was standing on the other side; and he was staring back at me with no words. I recognised him somehow, he was my father; even though I had not seen him for many years there was some feeling within that registered the fact that he was my father. I ran towards him and then he lifted me into the clouds. It was the best feeling ever; the foreign land had brought me a step closer to my father and my family – wow!

REFLECTIVE QUESTION

How might Awura Adjoa be feeling at being reunited with her family?

My father turned me around, lifted my arms up with so much excitement, his eyes beaming as he did this. It was as though he was examining me to see if there was any difference. I was so happy and yet I couldn't say much. The excitement was such that I became speechless. Mrs K and her husband came and joined us and we went inside. As I entered the house, I thought, wow! The inside of the house was different from what I had imagined all along. I mean, I wasn't ready for what I saw; this is where I would be living. It was definitely bigger than my auntie and uncle's one-bedroom rented accommodation that we lived in while in West Africa. My father showed me to my room and then I stopped and looked at him, and without me even asking he said, 'Everybody will be back home soon, they are all out at the moment'. I didn't realise how exhausted I was from all the travelling and the build-up of excitement. I needed rest and of course as Mrs K and my father spoke I fell asleep in his arms and he must have taken me up to my room and put me to bed.

The next thing I remember was waking up a few hours later to so much noise in the house. I was slightly scared because on waking up I realised I was in a different environment altogether and this time it wasn't Mrs K's house in West Africa where I had pizza for the first time nor was it the airport where our flight was cancelled, and it was definitely not Mrs K's house in the UK where I had tried grapes for the first time. I followed the noise downstairs. I was very careful and tried to be as quiet as possible. As I made my way down I saw faces that I had not seen before but one woman specifically stood looking at me. I didn't recognise her at all so I just stood there looking back at her. Then a tear dropped from her cheeks, she came towards me, hugged me and said, 'My child'. Others started to walk towards me and appeared eager to hug me. I felt so special; everybody wanted to touch me, everybody was smiling, and happy. I didn't know most of these people. There was food being cooked. I walked through the kitchen to the dining room, back to the living room, to the front door and then to the garden. I was so excited. There were so many people and I got introduced to everybody: 'That's your auntie, that's your uncle'; 'Uncle this'; 'This is auntie that'; 'That's grandmother'; 'That's grandpa'. There were so many names and titles that I didn't think I would remember everybody's name that day, but of course I knew that as time went on I would I get to know everybody so I wasn't too worried.

REFLECTIVE QUESTION

What are your views about the welcome given to Awura Adjoa on her arrival at her parents' house?

The days that followed consisted of being taken out to town to see the shopping centre and to purchase new clothes, tourist activities being planned by my parents for me to see places of interest and so on. These visits also involved visiting their church.

REFLECTIVE QUESTION

What in your opinion is the relevance of Awura Adjoa being taken to see the church as part of her introduction to the UK?

Back in West Africa, church was a big part of my life. I was raised a Christian, and even in the absence of my parents, my extended family ensured that I continued to take my faith seriously and this has continued until now. I remember being introduced to so many people at church, more people than at what I am now calling my welcome party at home, which was exciting and adventurous. Adventurous! That's what the trip had been so far, an adventure. A discovery of new things and new people, and each day I looked forward to discovering more things. As time went by I began to fit into the foreign land as I was enrolled into primary school (Year 6) and I was more than eager to adapt to my new environment, my family and my new life. Life as I knew it was perfect and nothing could go wrong. Well at least so it seemed.

Analysis

It is the view of Cunningham and Cunningham (2008, p 79), that the family *'is one of the core institutions in our society'* and that there are positive and negative characteristics associated with different family forms. They also suggest that there is no one universally agreed type of family. This corroborates the view by Parke (2013) that there is no such entity as an 'ideal' family and that there are emerging family forms which are useful to understand. It is suggested by Verhoef (2005) that in Sub-Saharan Africa, the term *family* has a connotation that goes beyond the notion of a biological mother, father and children. It extends to include many other relations and relationships such as *aunt, uncle, grandparent, brothers, sisters* and any other relatives who may be identified.

Awura Adjoa lived with her paternal uncle with no children while in West Africa, and on arrival in the UK would be living with her father, mother and siblings. The change in the type of family Awura Adjoa would be living in was perhaps a new experience for her and every effort should have been made to ensure she was confident about these changes.

The view that people older than yourself need to be accorded respect is a widely held one, more so in communities and families which view age as a defining factor in relationships (Twum-Danso Imoh, 2012). Children are required to include a prefix when addressing anyone older than themselves. So for example, *sister Grace, brother John* are not uncommon within some communities in the West African context. The use of the prefix *sister* and *brother* does not always denote a blood relationship.

It would appear that this system also prevailed within this family in the UK, when upon arrival various people were introduced to Awura Adjoa as *auntie* or *uncle*. It may be the case that for safeguarding reasons it is important to identify whether an *aunt* or *uncle* is indeed related by blood or someone who has been given this title by virtue of their age. This arbitrary system of identifying friends and relations could have far-reaching implications for children, particularly ones who are vulnerable and at risk of being abused and/or exploited.

Awura Adjoa is taken to the home of the chaperone on arrival in the UK and despite the length of time it had been since she saw her parents, there appeared to be no urgency to reunite her with them. What is more, the chaperone appeared to be acting with the agreement or knowledge of Awura Adjoa's parents; otherwise it is very likely that Awura Adjoa's parents would have picked her up from the care of the chaperone. The next day the chaperone drove her to her parents' house, contrary to the initial information that Awura Adjoa's parents would be coming to pick her up.

Writing specifically about Ghana, Twum-Danso Imoh (2012) identifies the key values of respect, obedience, humility, honesty, reliability and responsibility as guiding the strategies which most parents use to attempt to instil these values into their children.

REFLECTIVE QUESTIONS

From the preceding narrative, how would you describe or explain the sort of child Awura Adjoa is/was?

What are your views about the system of deference accorded to adults within the culture discussed above?

What are your views about Awura Adjoa being met and received at the airport by Mr K and not her parents?

FEELINGS AND LEARNING CHECK

Consider how the narrative contained in this chapter has made you feel.

Reflect on what you knew before and what you have learned from this chapter.

CHAPTER SUMMARY

In this chapter, Awura Adjoa has arrived in the UK and has been met by Mrs K's husband at the airport. She is excited to have come a step closer to reuniting with her parents. While the arrangements for getting her to her parents' home appeared to change, when she eventually arrives there they had planned a party to celebrate her arrival. Awura Adjoa is introduced to many relatives and family friends. She is also taken to see a few places of interest and the church.

FURTHER READING

Nzira, V (2011) Social Care with African Families in the UK. *London: Routledge.*

Therborn, G (2005) African Families in a Global Context *(NAI Research Reports). Uppsala: Nordic Africa Institute.*

3 Misunderstandings: the beginning of the worst

After what seemed like the longest journey I've ever taken, life as I knew it had changed. My days consisted of things such as doing chores just like I used to do in West Africa, helping out around the house, except this time it was in a foreign land. While I was no longer in Africa, I still was expected to be respectful and, being a girl, to be useful around the house. These were things that I was used to because this is how I was raised in Africa and so here in the UK, I perceived this to be what my parents would expect of me. I still remember the many compliments I received from my parents, family members and other family friends when they came round the house and would see me cleaning or after they had received a warm welcome and hospitality from me. They would frequently comment that I was well-mannered, polite and more hardworking than my siblings who were born and raised in the UK. I found it strange; I mean, I had grown up being smacked, hit or beaten when I did something wrong and out of fear of the rod, I made sure that I did more chores, was respectful to adults and behaved like a well-raised child both in and out of the house.

I also soon became aware that my 'mother' was actually my stepmother, which is contrary to what I had been made to believe all the years growing up in West Africa. While growing up in Africa and moving to live with one extended family member or the other, I was told that my father and mother both lived abroad, and as a child I had no reason to disbelieve what I was being told. However, one afternoon after I had been in the UK for a while, my father and my stepmother sat me down and told me that there was something they needed to tell me. They revealed to me that my birth mother had died when I was a baby. I was broken but with time accepted this as the truth and despite this new revelation I continued to view my stepmother as my mother and believed that this did not change how I related to her.

REFLECTIVE QUESTIONS

What are your views about the timing of the disclosure to Awura Adjoa about her birth mother?

Do you feel this disclosure was handled appropriately? What are your reasons for this view?

Like other children, irrespective of how well behaved, I sometimes got things wrong and these errors and mistakes soon became subject of conversation which later resulted in arguments between my parents. My stepmother would usually report my behaviour to my father when he came back from work. She would often base her criticism on the upbringing I received in West Africa while living with extended family. I used to be scared of what the consequences would be. However, my father would only call me aside and speak to me. After a while, these complaints and reporting became something that was happening on a daily basis.

Back in West Africa, I used to stay indoors when I had nothing to do. It was my way of staying out of trouble. I would prefer to sleep rather than go out to play with friends and possibly end up in a fight or sustaining an injury. Given that this strategy worked, I continued that habit when I arrived in the UK. Besides actively keeping out of trouble, on return from school when there wasn't much to do, I would have a nap. One day my stepmother reported to my father about how unusual my sleeping in the daytime was. My father called me aside to find out what this was about and whether there was anything wrong with me, and as per previous responses, I said there was nothing wrong. I perceived my father to be an easy man to get on with; he loved me and often I found him easier to talk to and more understanding than my stepmother. I thought the suspicion around my sleeping when I had nothing to do had been dropped but little did I know it hadn't been. My stepmother raised it repeatedly with my father, and due to the frequency of the complaints my father rang my uncle and auntie in West Africa to find out whether this had been happening while I was in West Africa. My uncle confirmed to my father that it was nothing to be concerned about and that taking a nap in the daytime was just what I did when I had nothing to do in the house, instead of being outside looking for trouble like so many other children.

I began to feel uncomfortable as a child; I remember being anxious all the time at home because I didn't want any other actions of mine to be misunderstood. As time went by I became forgetful. I was forgetting where I put things even after someone had told me seconds prior. I was so nervous and tried so hard to avoid getting into trouble that I was instead getting into more trouble. One day, after I finished washing the dishes in the kitchen, I put the sponge used to wash the dishes in the cupboard underneath the sink. I meant no harm when I did that; however, when my stepmother realised that I had done that, she was very angry and waited for my father to come back from work to report the incident to him. I was very scared, particularly as my stepmother made references to my behaviour being 'abnormal', and when my father came back from work she repeated those views to him.

REFLECTIVE QUESTION

Consider how else Awura Adjoa's stepmother could have expressed her concerns over some of Awura Adjoa's behaviour.

I was upstairs in my room when my father called me to come downstairs. I was scared, my hands were shaking. I could barely feel my legs. When I went down, my father asked me why I had put the sponge in the cabinet under the sink after I finished washing up. I told him there was no reason. The truth is there was no reason. He looked at me and tears began running down my cheeks. I was so scared, ashamed and just wanted to be in my room, on my own. As it was late my father told me to go to my room. With reports and complaints about me every day I began to isolate myself from everyone. At least when I could, I tried to stay away from everyone.

REFLECTIVE QUESTION

Can you propose reasons for why Awura Adjoa's stepmother did not address any of her concerns personally with Awura Adjoa and instead passed these through Awura Adjoa's father?

After a while, my stepmother and father started to argue whenever I was the subject of their discussion. That made me feel even worse and my stepmother began to withdraw from me. She would make sure I was provided for, but began to avoid being close to me. The warmth and closeness I felt from her when I first came was no longer there. I was no longer happy at home. I looked forward to leaving the house to go to school just to avoid being around my stepmother. It got worse when my stepmother started to tell other 'aunties' and 'uncles' about what I had supposedly done and I would get chastised for it by others.

REFLECTIVE QUESTION

How might the notion of *family* have contributed to 'aunties' and 'uncles' feeling able to and responsible for commenting on Awura Adjoa's behaviour?

The worst came when I started to occasionally wet my bed. I couldn't help being incontinent of urine some nights and this became the subject of further anger and frustration from my stepmother.

One day, she became so angry at me about bedwetting so much that it became the basis of an argument between her and my father and they began to argue. I recall one occasion when, after I had been incontinent of urine, I was so scared that I took my pyjamas off on waking up early in the morning and hid them under my bed so no one would see them. I left them there for about two days and unfortunately for me, my stepmother found them there. She got so angry at me that when my father came back from work she told him about it. He was disappointed with me and I felt so ashamed. I told him I was scared of them finding out I had wet the bed and so I hid the wet clothes. I told him I didn't want to be smacked. My stepmother made a remark about how unusual my behaviour was and before she could say anything else, my father asked me to go upstairs to bed. That night in particular, I could hear them arguing in their room from my room. From what I could hear of the argument, my father was disagreeing with whatever my stepmother was saying.

The days that followed consisted of further arguments between my parents, creating a tense atmosphere. I looked forward to going to bed because that seemed the only free time where I didn't have to be scared or careful of what I did and said. Going to school was an escape route for me too. So that is what life swiftly became for me. Home became a place where I preferred not to be, and when I was out, I felt as free as a bird. My behaviour as a child had become something I was constantly cautious of because somehow it was causing problems, problems which did not even need to exist, and unknown to me were about to escalate even further.

 ## Analysis

In this chapter we become aware of the deteriorating relationship between Awura Adjoa and her parents in general and in particular, her stepmother. This analysis will focus on the themes of bedwetting, family disagreements, escape from home and emotional abuse.

It would appear that Awura Adjoa could not do anything to please her stepmother, to the point where her carers in West Africa were blamed for what she considered a poor upbringing. Her stepmother had started to report Awura Adjoa to her father for her forgetfulness and for taking a nap during the day.

The link between childhood incontinence and being labelled a witch has been acknowledged elsewhere (Bahunga, 2013; Tedam, 2014, 2016); however, it is critical to understand why such a link is important and what might be done to prevent the ongoing misconception within some communities that nocturnal enuresis in children is an indicator of witchcraft.

It is not clear whether or not the school were aware of Awura Adjoa's bedwetting, nor indeed whether she had been taken to the GP by her parents for further investigation. Al-Zaben and Sehlo (2015) suggest that the cost to parents for their children's bedwetting include additional washing as well as smell and odour in the home; however, they also caution that the use of punitive approaches are not only unhelpful but can have an adverse psychological impact on children. They claim that bedwetting can also result in a loss of self-esteem and the development of depression in children. Consequently, parents are advised to adopt a more caring and sensitive approach when trying to address their children's bedwetting.

Redsell and Collier (2000) comment on the inconvenience to parents resulting in them becoming intolerant of their children who are bedwetting. It could be suggested that the home environment led to Awura Adjoa feeling unhappy and unsafe and this could have resulted in the onset of bedwetting, especially as research by Al-Zaben and Sehlo (2015) suggests that fear and anxiety can cause bedwetting. Nocturnal enuresis had not been an issue while Awura Adjoa lived in West Africa and so it is plausible to conclude that a range of factors such as transitions, fear and anxiety may have contributed to this situation.

The repercussions of bedwetting were real and present; consequently, Awura Adjoa had started to use strategies which she felt would keep her out of trouble.

Awura Adjoa experienced the loss of a familiar environment and ways of doing things. There is little indication that her parents offered her any kind of formal 'induction' into the new country, home and way of doing things. Added to this, Awura Adjoa had recently become aware that her mother was actually her stepmother. For a ten-year-old, these issues appeared to have more of an effect than may have been acknowledged.

Disagreements and arguments occur in every family among the different people who make up the unit (sibling–sibling; parents–sibling; parent–parent). Families are '*organisationally complex*' (Connolly et al, 2006, p 77) and are interdependent and so any disagreements between its members affect the family as a whole. There is a sense that adult members of a family have the responsibility of supporting the emotional, social and physical well-being of children and young people within their families. The arguments within Awura Adjoa's household are not unique; however, the fact that Awura Adjoa had become aware that she was the source of the arguments between her parents was unfortunate and unhelpful. For a child to feel responsible for adult disagreements no doubt compounded her fear and anxiety to the point where she '*couldn't feel*' her legs.

Awura Adjoa sought sanctuary outside the family home and found school to be a particularly safe and peaceful environment. She comments on trying to be invisible by keeping out of her stepmother's way.

Twum-Danso (2012) argues that in many parts of West Africa a *good* child is perceived as one who does not answer back or question adults. This could be why Awura Adjoa never appeared to challenge or argue with her parents about complaints and allegations made against her.

Providing insight into some of the factors that shape parenting, Kotchick and Forehand (2002) argue that parenting practices that have elements of positive reinforcement, warmth and affection contribute to positive child outcomes characterised by high self-esteem, academic competence and positive peer relations. Conversely, practices that include openly harsh discipline, inconsistent, passive and emotionally vacant parenting is detrimental to the well-being of children and the outcomes are generally less positive.

Altomare et al (2005), writing about the differential treatment given to siblings by parents, cautions parents to ensure that any differential treatment between siblings should be aimed at harnessing difference in talent and personality, not for punitive reasons that culminate in unequal outcomes.

Doyle and Timms (2014) outline a series of carer and parental behaviour which constitute emotional abuse and neglect. These include corrupting, degrading, isolating, tormenting and rejecting children, as well as inducing a sense of fear and giving them inappropriate roles both within the home and outside. Rejection, for example, can be active or inactive and the evidence provided within this narrative confirms that Awura Adjoa experienced inactive rejection where her stepmother failed to show appreciation and warmth. Awura Adjoa was also tormented through the regular reporting of her behaviour and activities to her father on his return from work. Tormenting is closely linked to fear inducement, where the very thought of her actions being reported to her father would create a feeling of fear and insecurity about how her father would react to what he was told by Awura Adjoa's stepmother.

In some ethnic minority communities and within some homes, discipline of children rests with the father or male elder within the home (Hauari and Hollingworth, 2009) and we see some of this through Awura Adjoa's experiences. It has been argued that what accounts for this gendered form of discipline is predicated on patriarchal systems of hierarchy within families. It was refreshing that Awura Adjoa felt her father was a fair man and that he adopted a non-threatening method of open discussion to raise the stepmother's concerns with Awura Adjoa and to gain her views about what she perceived was going on. In addition, Awura Adjoa's father is said to have consulted her auntie and uncle in West Africa with the view to understanding whether or not Awura Adjoa's behaviour was consistent with what they had experienced of her while she lived with them. It could be suggested that this was a helpful strategy which would lay to rest any doubts or suspicions arising from Awura Adjoa's daytime napping and her bedwetting.

FEELINGS AND LEARNING CHECK

Consider how the narrative contained in this chapter has made you feel.

Reflect on what you knew before and what you have learned from this chapter.

CHAPTER SUMMARY

In this chapter, we are introduced to some of the difficulties Awura Adjoa is beginning to experience. She has become forgetful, has occasional naps during the day when she is not busy and has started to wet the bed at night. We read that her stepmother does not take this well and has started to report her to her father on his return from work. Awura Adjoa begins to find safety and peace in school and this appears to buffer the effect of her home experiences.

FURTHER READING

Bahunga, J (2013) Tackling Child Abuse Linked to Faith or Belief. Every Child Journal, *3(3): 14–19.*

Doyle, C and Timms, C (2014) Child Neglect and Emotional Abuse: Understanding, Assessment and Response. London: Sage.

4   Labelled and tainted

Growing up in West Africa, I used to watch African movies with adults and children alike. Some of these movies followed storylines which had ritualistic themes and undertones and often featured people who visited these ritualists for charms and powers which turned them into witches. For me at the age of ten, what I knew about witchcraft was what I saw in these films. I never imagined the word would become a reality for me and that it would be a label people would associate me with.

On many occasions, my stepmother found reason to believe that my behaviour was strange and abnormal. She made that quite clear and really and truly, that was the beginning of being labelled. It was not long before the discussions she had with my father about me became more focused on suggestions that I was possessed. One day, I overheard her saying that I sometimes looked like I was not in my own body and that I was forgetful. As days turned into weeks and the weeks turned into months, these discussions became reasons for argument between my parents. My father, who was a man of God himself, assured my stepmother that he had no reason to believe that I was possessed. These disagreements consequently led to further arguments and disagreements between them. My stepmother began to make constant remarks to me about me being the reason why her and my father constantly argued and accused me of trying to ruin their marriage. I would cry myself to sleep at night, feeling bad and believing that she was right and that I was the reason why they argued. As time went on, I became more and more isolated both at home and at school. I looked forward to going to school as it seemed the only place where I would go alone and be in control of what I did without worrying about it being a problem. Church was a place I went to with a fake smile on my face, while deep down I cried for someone to comfort me but there was no one.

I recall an incident at my grandmother's house which had disastrous outcomes for me. She had a nice view from her window so as children we would sit on the window ledge and admire the view. One day, my little sister came to join me as I sat on the window ledge, quietly looking out. I didn't speak much to her at that moment because I was in a world of my own. As she sat next to me I reached out to hold her just as my older sister walked into that area of the house we were in. She rushed to my little sister and grabbed her off the window ledge where we sat. I was confused. I also then climbed down off the ledge and as I did so she ran to the living room where my stepmother, grandmother, and some of my aunties and uncles were and the next thing I heard was her telling them that I was attempting to throw my little sister out of the window. I started crying immediately, uncontrollable tears rolling down my cheeks.

I walked into the living room, only to be the focus of everyone's gaze. My stepmother began to question me about why I was trying to throw my little sister out of the window. I was speechless. I wanted the ground to open up and take me in and I didn't know what to say; even worse, I had nothing to say. Everyone was looking at me. All I did was cry. My stepmother came towards me, pulled my ears really hard and repeated the question. I held onto the hand she was using to pull my ears as it was ever so painful. Then she said the word. In my native language she called out the word witch. I began crying even louder and harder. Some of the aunties in the living room came to my rescue while I cried. I recall one of my aunties shouting at my mother telling her to stop, as she and other family members continued to make remarks about me being a witch. This auntie came to my rescue by taking me upstairs to one of the rooms to console me. I don't think I have ever cried so much in my life. I never imagined that there could be any day that would be worse than that day. For me, that one word had changed not only that day but also the weeks ahead for me. As I stayed in the room the rest of the family were downstairs talking. I didn't hear what they were talking about but I knew for sure it was about me. I stayed in the room where I continued to cry. My auntie brought food for me later on, which I ate. After a while, I came downstairs and even though no one said anything regarding what had happened, there was tension in the atmosphere. I stayed in the living room where we all watched TV.

Later that evening, my father came from work and met us at my grandmother's. When my father walked through the door, I was scared to go and welcome him. I worried that he might ignore or reject me. I knew he was going to be given more information which was likely to make him view me differently. All the other children and some of the adults met him at the door to welcome him in; while they embraced him, he asked about me: 'Where is Awura Adjoa?' My cousin muttered to him that I was in the living room. I heard him ask about me so I had started to make my way to the front door when he met me at the entrance of the living room. 'Hello baby girl, how are you?' he asked. I replied saying I was fine, but he knew something was wrong. I didn't say anything and just made my way back into the living room and he followed me. He came in and greeted the rest of the family and sat down. The aunties and uncles started a random conversation with him and didn't mention anything in particular. He was given something to eat and then as my heart pounded loudly only to myself, my stepmother narrated the incident of the day. Tears began to roll down my cheeks as I sat and listened to them in shock and disbelief. I was so ashamed. My father called me by name and asked why I had tried to push my sister out of the window. With tears rolling down my cheeks I replied, 'No reason'. No reason... That was what I said because I didn't see the point of arguing and saying that it was not what had happened.

REFLECTIVE QUESTIONS

Why do you think Awura Adjoa responded to her father in the way she did when she was asked about the incident involving her younger sister?

How might her father have interpreted her response?

Conclusions had been drawn; there was no hope for me and that's why I said 'no reason'. I felt I had been found guilty without being given the opportunity to explain or defend myself. Who would listen to me anyway? My father did not really have anything further to say to me after my response. My stepmother added this to her rationale for believing I was possessed. I listened to the conclusion: I was a witch, possessed and here to cause harm and damage to members of my own family. I was in tears; I'm not sure whether the tears made a difference but it was the only emotion I could manage. Tears seemed to be my only response in the preceding days and weeks. I sat and listened as I was told I was a witch. My siblings and cousins looked at me differently. I was ashamed. I didn't have anything to say because even if I did, who would listen? One of my aunties asked all the children to go upstairs and we all obliged. While upstairs the demarcation was immediate and clear. I noticed that all the other children stayed away from me. I sat alone in one corner of the room with nothing else than my thoughts, fears, pain and sadness. After some time my father called for me and my siblings and told us to start getting ready and that we were going home. I finally made my way downstairs, put my coat on, and said my goodbyes to the rest of the family. We made our way home and just like many other nights I looked forward to getting into bed.

The days that followed continued to be eventful; my stepmother and my father constantly argued about me. I would look forward to waking up and getting ready for school and each morning as I walked out of the house for school I felt my insides lighten up. I would feel a sense of relief. However, while in school I continued to isolate myself so things had not really changed that much. I was still the African girl in school who had funny hair and had an accent and there was some teasing and making fun of me, but that was minimal in comparison to what I was facing at home. I became more and more isolated in school and things deteriorated to a point where I would sit in my lessons and could not stop cry- ing. I didn't mean to. My peers would sometimes laugh at me for crying for no apparent reason or for occasionally staring into thin air. My teachers would ask if I was OK. I would say yes and they would tell me to ignore my peers who laughed and made fun of me, as in the students who had been laughing at me. My peers? She thought my worry or the reason for my tears was because of the bullies. She made that assumption and had told other teachers that. I was scared to say anything because I didn't want her to inform or approach my parents. I wished on so many occasions that I could tell her that I was accused of being a witch. I hesitated because I didn't think she would understand. I had been labelled, and that was bad enough. I didn't want the situation compounded by her talking to my parents about my demeanour in school. Sadly, despite not disclosing to my teachers what was going on at home, things were about to get worse for me.

Analysis

It is the case that schools deal with large numbers of children at any given time and so it can be easy to miss children who may be at risk of harm or who may be presenting as being in need of support and protection and who have not disclosed their concerns to staff. This chapter has acknowledged the low-level bullying that may have been going on in Awura Adjoa's school; however, for the children who appeared to find Awura Adjoa 'strange' it must have been difficult for them to embrace their peer who had not long arrived from Africa and who (in their view) cried for no reason. Although teachers appeared to have misunderstood and misinterpreted what was going on for Awura Adjoa, it is still fairly frustrating that they told her to 'ignore the bullies'. The discussion here focuses on other ways in which the teachers could have addressed *bullying*. By telling Awura Adjoa to '*ignore the bullies*', the burden of intervention or non-intervention was left with Awura Adjoa, which for a ten-year-old does not seem appropriate. It is argued here that if the teacher(s) concerned had attempted to address the perceived bullying, it may have led them to the actual cause of Awura Adjoa's demeanour and presentation in school. Links between bullying and longer-term negative effects have been shown (Tucker and Maunder, 2015). It has also been suggested that teachers are often left to decide whether to intervene in cases of bullying, and also to decide on the nature of the intervention based on whether they perceive the bullying to be more or less severe.

Persistent crying in lesson time and staring vaguely into the air should have raised sufficient concern; however, it is still important that in the event of a concern around bullying then relationship-building activities and intervention between Awura Adjoa and her peers would have been useful and welcome. That Awura Adjoa did not feel able to speak to her teachers about what was going on at home could suggest that teachers need to be able to build trust with their pupils and assist them to understand how any concerns disclosed will be handled. It is possible that such a process may have encouraged Awura Adjoa to disclose her experiences at home.

Awura Adjoa was being accused of attempting to harm her younger sister by pushing her out of a window. This suspicion resulted in Awura Adjoa being repeatedly accused, quizzed and interrogated about whether or not she was a witch. The reaction of the family members is interesting to analyse. Only one adult appeared to care about how Awura Adjoa was feeling and subsequently provided some comfort. Awura Adjoa's cousins and siblings surprisingly went along with the adults and immediately stayed away from her. The picture that is created is of a divide with Awura Adjoa on her own on the one side, and the others on the other. For any child, such obvious ostracising would be humiliating and embarrassing. The effect of the label resulted in a loss of status for Awura Adjoa, which according to Link and Phelan (2001) would have been likely to have resulted in her being perceived as less attractive to socialise with or be seen to associate with. It is also interesting that the other children appeared to understand the concept of witchcraft.

Worthy of consideration is how her half-sister may have understood the allegation against Awura Adjoa, and given that she was younger than Awura Adjoa, whether she felt able to provide a different explanation of what had occurred.

It would appear that Awura Adjoa had prior knowledge of witchcraft from watching videos and TV programmes while in West Africa. This is consistent with the view put forward by Asamoah-Gyadu (2015), that witchcraft in Africa is reinforced through films and movies which depict the cause of death, suffering and ill health as being due to witchcraft. In addition, it could be argued that children in Africa and in African families are familiar with the concept of witchcraft through the process of socialisation.

FEELINGS AND LEARNING CHECK

Consider how the narrative contained in this chapter has made you feel.

Reflect on what you knew before and what you have learned from this chapter.

CHAPTER SUMMARY

In this chapter, Awura Adjoa shared an experience which occurred at her step-grandmother's house. She was accused of attempting to push her half-sister out of a window as they sat together on the window ledge enjoying the beautiful view. This accusation resulted in her being labelled a witch and also created an immediate wedge between her and the other children who were present.

FURTHER READING

Asamoah-Gyadu, J K (2015) Witchcraft Accusations and Christianity in Africa. International Bulletin of Missionary Research, *39(1): 23–27.*

Link, B G and Phelan, J C (2001) Conceptualising Stigma. Annual Review of Sociology, *27: 363–85.*

5   Confess you must

My father had always cared about me, and I never doubted that he loved me. Even with everything that was going on, while I felt ashamed by the fact that he came home tired from work every day only to get negative reports of me, I still felt he cared about my welfare. I believed that was the reason why he and my stepmother argued so frequently. Things became more heated at home between them, as they constantly argued. When outside I smiled and looked happy and also portrayed the perfect image of the family to 'outsiders', while inside at home, I curled up in my shell with the only person I could confide in and who believed in my innocence – me.

My siblings at home appeared to relate well with me although I noticed a little change but did not think too much of it at the time. I had older siblings who were at university the majority of the time; however, when they were home they were fairly OK with me even after I was labelled a witch. My stepmother did not want me to ever be left alone with my younger sibling and it was clear that she believed I was a witch. I remained the subject of conversation between my stepmother and my father and the focus of their arguments. I was scared and hurt because the mother–daughter relationship I thought we had was deteriorating. She did the bare minimum for me and the emotional connection no longer existed.

I woke up one day to what seemed like a meeting between myself and my parents. I remember being so afraid. I stood in front of them with my hands behind my back as a sign of respect. My father asked me if I was OK, and I responded and said I was fine. I was very polite with my responses, saying 'Yes please' or 'Sorry, no' depending on what the question was. My father regularly asked me how I was and although this appeared to be happening more frequently than before, I thought nothing of it. It sounded as though he was concerned about me.

One evening I was told that we were going to go to church, and so I made sure I completed my house chores and everything else in order to be ready in good time. Going to church services midweek was something my parents did on their own while us kids were left at home because they said we had school the next day, and so it was a rare occurrence for them to take us to midweek church service. However, on this occasion, I didn't think much of it and saw it as one of those rare occurrences that I was accompanying them to their weekly service which took place at our church where we were regular members. We made our way to the church and when we arrived, I realised it wasn't our usual church. This was a new church.

REFLECTIVE QUESTION

What are your views about Awura Adjoa's parents asking her to attend church with them on a school night, outside their usual practice?

I remember going down some stairs, which took us to what was like a basement where the service took place. Going down the stairs it felt like going underground. I didn't think much of it. All I thought was that we were going to a church service. When we arrived that evening, I remember my parents going to speak to a man who appeared to be the pastor. They asked me to sit and wait for them and so I sat down on the chair in one part of the room, while they went and spoke to him. After speaking to him for some time, my father turned and beckoned to me. I went towards them and as I approached, the pastor asked me how I was, speaking in a native language I understood. He smiled and shook his head and then he asked me if I was a witch. I remember becoming instantly confused thinking in my head, 'Oh no', this is why we are here. I responded to him saying, 'No', I was not a witch. He chuckled and then told my parents to pray with him. They formed a circle around me, with me in the middle and they screamed out at the top of their voices praying.

As they continued to pray, tears rolled down my cheeks. I was hurting inside and felt nothing but pain and sadness. All I could do was cry. I had been wearing a coat since I left the house and had become quite warm so began to take my jacket off; they continued to pray loudly and I kept on crying. The pastor stopped and asked me what I was doing, and I told him that I was hot so I was taking my jacket off. My parents had opened their eyes at this point and I stared up at the pastor in front of me. Speaking in a language I understood, he asked, 'Are you hot? You haven't seen anything yet'. I looked at him, so confused, and just then he went to my parents and told them not to worry and that in a few days I was going to confess to being a witch! I looked on as my parents nodded their heads in acknowledgement. Tears continued to roll down my cheeks.

REFLECTIVE QUESTIONS

Can you visualise the situation that has just been described?

What can you see in your mind's eye and how would you describe this?

THE EXORCISM EXPERIENCE

© Harry Venning

'Confess to what? What exactly would I be confessing to?' I thought to myself. It became clear to me that this pastor had informed my parents that I was a witch. I stood there, lost in my thoughts, as the pastor continued to speak to my parents, saying to them that I had been 'given something'. I understood that 'something' to mean witchcraft. Before I could contemplate any further, he then said directly in my local language that I have been 'given' witchcraft. That's when I felt like I had been punched in the stomach. Once again the 'W' word, and from a pastor. My mind went blank. All I felt at that moment was pain. Crying was the only thing that I was able to do and nothing was happening around me that made sense to me. I felt very confused.

REFLECTIVE QUESTIONS

Can you identify areas of the preceding narrative where threatening language and/or behaviour was used/directed towards Awura Adjoa?

What are your views about this?

The next thing I remember was getting home. I cannot even recollect being able to speak after that revelation in church. I remember feeling so hot. I had what would medically be termed a temperature. I went upstairs and changed into my pyjamas as I did every night. I just wanted to get into my bed to sleep. As I got changed my father came into my room and gave me a Bible which had been opened at a scripture and directed me to place it under my pillow as I slept. I obliged, put the Bible under my pillow and got into bed to sleep. I was awake for a while when I got into bed and could hear my stepmother and father's voices coming from their bedroom. I covered my head and all I did was cry, cry myself to sleep.

 Analysis

The visit to the church and the availability of the pastor could not have been coincidental. The entire visit appeared to have been pre-planned and it is quite clear from the pastor's behaviour and attitude that he had been made aware of the family's concerns in regard to Awura Adjoa. This prior information could have been used to safeguard Awura Adjoa and protect her from harm and trauma, in that the pastor could have arranged a very different type of 'intervention', which perhaps involved counselling or talking to Awura Adjoa and her parents about some of the behaviours they perceived as odd. At the very least and perhaps in line with the kind of faith that many subscribe to, the pastor could have prayed for Awura Adjoa in absentia. She did not need to be present, especially as it was a school night. It is not clear whether this special arrangement, outside of the standard church hours, was paid for; however, it is clear that, on the part of Awura Adjoa's parents, the aim of the visit was to 'confirm' their allegations. The pastor concludes that Awura Adjoa is indeed a witch and that she had been 'given' witchcraft. Agbanusi (2016) has suggested that believers in witchcraft state that witchcraft can be acquired in later life or in some cases people are born with it. The pastor's comment is therefore suggestive of the fact that Awura Adjoa's witchcraft was 'acquired'.

It is unclear whether the actions of the pastor and Awura Adjoa's family would constitute exorcism as has been described earlier on in the book. At the very least, the action of three adults putting hands over a child and praying loudly does evidence the use and display of power, which appears to have exacerbated Awura Adjoa's anxiety.

It is also significant to note that when Awura Adjoa took her coat off because she was feeling hot, the meaning associated with that action was one that inadvertently fed into the pastor's conclusion. A focus on the process Awura Adjoa had to undergo and the pastor's declaration that she was indeed a witch requires further analysis.

Cohan (2011, p 853) suggests that *'witchcraft accusations are often fuelled by charismatic or Pentecostal churches that stand to profit from treatment offered to exorcise people, including children, who are identified as witches'*. We are not in the position to state either way whether this pastor was remunerated for his services with this family; however, this notion of remuneration is meaningful and relevant to our understanding.

It has been argued by Humphrey (2015) that rituals held in some Pentecostal churches around the world are used to exorcise 'evil' from children. The concept of exorcism is a complicated area to attempt to rehearse here, especially as the description provided by Awura Adjoa has a loose 'fit' with the concept. That said, the aim of this book is to create awareness of the different forms of abuse that arise when children are labelled witches and to support practitioners to recognise and take appropriate action to safeguard children. For this reason, it is expedient to suggest that the process of three adults surrounding any child while shouting (prayers or otherwise) can be frightening and uncomfortable for a child and constitutes emotional abuse.

Writing from a legal perspective, Hall (2016) notes that a person cannot consent to the actual bodily harm that is often associated with exorcism. With regards to children, we argue that they cannot consent to their own abuse and/or exploitation under any circumstance; consequently, abuse is abuse and the guidelines for dealing with these sorts of situations are outlined in various legal and policy frameworks (eg DfE, 2015).

On her return home, Awura Adjoa retired to bed and was given a Bible, and was asked to leave it open and place it under her pillow. Awura Adjoa did not look at the section of the biblical scripture she was given by her father to place under her pillow so we are unable to comment on the value/importance of that action. Nonetheless, what we can reflect upon is why Awura Adjoa's father chose not to discuss the relevance of this action with his daughter. It is important to note that Awura Adjoa obliged, without question, again consistent with the view of Twum-Danso Imoh (2012) about African children socialised into systems where it is considered rude and inappropriate to question or challenge the actions of adults.

The next day I woke up quite fearful, not knowing what to expect. And rightly so, because what followed was emotional and physical distance from everyone. I was not sure whether my siblings had been told the details of what had transpired the day before, but as I knew it I was now the 'witch' in the house. In the days that followed, I would go to school, sit in lessons, but not really pay attention and I was unable to concentrate. Most days, what ran through my mind was the 'W' word. I was practically just an empty shell, not an ounce of joy inside of me. Outside and in public I would smile, as would my stepmother and father, acting as though nothing had happened, but at home I was going through what seemed like hell. At school, I avoided talking about home or making friends because at home, I was a witch. My father worked long hours in the day and at night and my relationship with him appeared to be going downhill very quickly, and it was clear that he had finally also taken on the view that I was a witch. It wasn't long before other members of the family were formally notified that I was a witch and that the pastor had confirmed it. The pastor's evidence was the final nail that sealed my coffin because previous discussions had been more accusatory but suddenly the confirmation by the pastor had turned these allegations and suspicions into some sort of reality.

REFLECTIVE QUESTIONS

What do you think was the purpose of Awura Adjoa's parents 'formally notifying' other members of the family that Awura Adjoa was a witch?

What do you consider to be the repercussions of this action?

People's relationship with me within the family quickly changed and I was not oblivious to it. Another example of the bad treatment I received came when one night while I was in bed asleep, my stepmother woke me up at midnight and told me to come out of my room. She had a wooden spoon in her hand which she was waving around in the air. The wooden spoon was used to hit me repeatedly. She started saying in our African language that it was midnight and she knows that in spirit I was about to go and meet with other witches and that was why she woke me up at that time to make my confession. I was in tears and I kept repeating the fact that I was not a witch. I had been woken up from sleep. I was told to confess to being a witch. And no matter how many times I said I was not a witch, my stepmother was not prepared to leave me alone. She waved the wooden spoon in the air, hitting me on and off with it, telling me I must confess. I continued crying, yelling out that I was not a witch, but she told me that I was not going to go to bed until I had told the truth. I repeatedly kept telling her that I was not a witch, which was the truth, but she continued to say I was lying.

After almost an hour, it was clear that there was only one way for me to go to bed and that was by simply saying I was a witch. I reckoned that this would let her leave me alone. As I stood there crying and being shouted at, a wooden spoon being waved in my face, I uttered the words which I knew would set me free to go back to bed. 'OK, I'm a witch', I said. She asked me to repeat what I had just said. I thought that would mean I would finally get to go back to bed, and as I waited for her to finally give me the permission to go to bed, she asked, 'Who gave this witchcraft to you?' 'Oh my God, I have just made things worse', I thought to myself. I had already lied just so all of this could end and the tone with which she had asked the question was a lot softer than the tone she had been using earlier so I thought I had to keep the lie going. I said I did not know, and she raised the wooden spoon as if to hit me with it. Without thinking about it, I blurted out the name of the relative I had been staying with in West Africa. What had I done? I had lied. But it seemed to have worked. She put the wooden spoon down and left me standing for a while. This whole process had gone on for approximately two hours.

REFLECTIVE QUESTION

Reflecting on what you know about emotional abuse, how might you summarise the impact of this event on Awura Adjoa?

She came back later and asked me to go to bed. I went into my room, closed my door and looked at myself in the mirror. My eyes were so swollen and I felt self-pity. The image I saw of myself while looking in the mirror made me cry even more. I cried even more as I got into bed and could not sleep. After a while I heard footsteps approaching my room and so I snuggled under the duvet on my bed, closed my eyes and pretended to be asleep. I then felt a presence of someone standing over me and watching me, and then as the person turned and walked out of my room I opened one eye to see who it was and saw it was my stepmother. She closed the door behind her and I opened my eyes. I did not go back to sleep after that. I was so wide awake and all I did was cry.

The morning came and I stayed in bed and didn't want to come out of my room. I had heard my father return from work that morning and I had heard him and my stepmother talking. It was inevitable that my father was going to call me and question me. I knew he would have been told what had transpired during the night. I got out of bed when I heard my father calling me; I went to his room and started to feel my palms become sweaty. He asked me what had happened that night. My stepmother sat next to him in bed and I knew she would have told him everything. I began to narrate to my father what had happened, telling him how I had been woken up from sleep, the questioning, the wooden spoon and how I repeatedly said that I was not a witch. Then my father asked me if I was a witch and I said 'no'. In that instance my stepmother gazed at me and she yelled out, saying that it wasn't the truth and that I had already confessed to being a witch. With tears running down my cheeks, I told her that I had said that to her so she would allow me to return to bed. I added that I thought that was what she wanted to hear because when I was telling the truth about not being a witch she had repeatedly said that I was lying.

REFLECTIVE QUESTIONS

Why do you think it was important for Awura Adjoa's stepmother to secure a confession from Awura Adjoa?

What are your views on her stepmother's 'strategy' to coerce Awura Adjoa to confess to being a witch?

My father turned and looked at my stepmother in the bed. He asked me to go and get ready for school, and I did. That morning felt different; I still didn't feel relieved after leaving the house. I had not slept, and while I was in school that day I kept dozing off. I tried to make sure I stayed awake. That day my teacher noticed that I looked a bit unwell and she asked me to go and see the school nurse in the sick bay. I obliged and went to the school nurse, who after checking me over recommended that she would call my parents to come and pick me up. I recall jumping out of the chair I was sitting in and told her that I was well enough for the day, and that there was no one at home anyway. She stared at me for a while and then asked my classteacher for her opinion and she suggested for me to be given my work to do in a separate space so I would not be disturbed by the other children. That sounded good enough for me. Going home was not an option and I was happy with the decision both my school nurse and my classteacher had made.

REFLECTIVE QUESTIONS

Do you think the school nurse and/or the teacher could have done any more than they did?

What could they have done and what are your reasons for this view?

There wasn't much to do that day for me at home, and the days and weeks that followed were made up of my stepmother throwing comments about me being a witch and not wanting me to do anything for her, not even the chores in the house. I should have felt relieved that I was no longer doing house chores, but I wasn't. The reason why I wasn't doing house chores was because I was tainted. I had been forced to confess to being something that I wasn't. It was evident in the days that followed that my stepmother was not happy with the fact that after all that happened that night, I still maintained the truth, my truth, that I was not a witch.

Analysis

In this chapter, there is evidence of physical abuse in the use of the wooden spoon, which was used to repeatedly hit Awura Adjoa and coerce her into a confession. Physical abuse is a safeguarding concern and should not be tolerated under any circumstances. Research suggests that there are disproportionate numbers of black African children in the looked after systems of care in the UK, largely due to physical abuse (Bernard and Gupta, 2008), and so it is fair to conclude that contemporary practice would have resulted in a robust assessment and the family may have found themselves in a difficult situation.

It is also recognised that waking Awura Adjoa up at midnight is neglectful behaviour which should be challenged by practitioners. The timeline identified through this section of the narrative indicates this confrontation occurred around 12 midnight until around 2am. Awura Adjoa's stepmother, in not recognising Awura Adjoa's need for rest and sleep, had engaged in neglectful and abusive parenting. In this context, neglect is taken to mean parents or caregivers ignoring a child's needs. According to Awura Adjoa, her stepmother offered the view that she had chosen this time because '*it was midnight and she knows that in spirit I was about to go and meet with other witches and that was why she woke me up at that time*'. Again, this belief by Awura Adjoa's stepmother is consistent with the findings by Levack (2014) that witches would avail themselves at '*nocturnal assemblies*' (p 926) where they would meet to plan harm. Similarly, Adinkrah (2004) suggests that witches are considered to have mystical powers which enable them to leave the body of the witch and join other witches in the spirit world, where the aim is to wreak havoc and to inflict harm on unsuspecting innocent people. These types of beliefs may account for Awura Adjoa's stepmother's position and her utterances about her rationale for waking Awura Adjoa up at midnight. According to Cohan (2011), by self-incriminating, Awura Adjoa had unknowingly made things worse.

Awura Adjoa was being verbally and physically tormented regularly through the frequent questioning, isolation and making her feel unloved and unwanted. Her constant sobbing will not have been in her best interest (Doyle and Timms, 2014).

Emotionally, Awura Adjoa was constantly reminded that she was unloved, worthless and evil. She was also constantly on edge, anxious and fearful of what would happen next. All these, according to Davies and Duckett (2016), constitute emotional abuse and impact negatively on children's self-worth.

For many ten-year-old children, the thought of doing household chores is not always welcome and can be a source of upset within a home. In Awura Adjoa's case, a cultural lens must be used to understand the rejection and disappointment she felt at not being allowed to undertake any chores at home. It would be unfair to suggest that all children from a particular region of the world are encouraged to do home chores; however, it has been suggested by Nzira (2011) that children from African backgrounds are expected to help their parents within the home with chores and in some instances to look after younger siblings and relatives. Taking this into account would demonstrate that Awura Adjoa considered doing chores a privilege, which was subsequently withdrawn following being labelled as a witch. On a similar note, Awura Adjoa's parents must have known what her reaction to being de-privileged would have been and the impact this would have had on her. I argue here that this knowledge of cultural norms and behaviours strengthened their position of power all the more by making it clear that Awura Adjoa's help around the house was neither welcome nor sought after.

After the summer holidays, I started a new school as I had gone from primary to secondary school. The excitement of starting secondary school kept me happy and I looked forward to the experience. My experiences at home continued to be the same and my parents regularised our visits to the church, taking me to every service irrespective of the day or time. The fact that I had school the following day seemed not to have mattered and instead it appeared important that I was taken to every service that took place at church. I never thought much about it, especially because it was our usual church and not the other pastor's church where I had been labelled a witch. One evening during midweek service, I was so tired that I was dozing off sitting next to my parents at church. My stepmother woke me up and took me outside where she told me off for sleeping and said in my local language that I was sleeping at church because I was a witch. She told me to stay awake and partake in the prayers since that would help draw out the evil spirit within me. It was at that point that I realised that the reason for the new pattern of bringing me to every service taking place at church was because they believed I was a witch. It was clearly so that, in her own words, the witchcraft in me could be drawn out through prayer. My notion of going to church changed at this point. While the pastor at our usual church seemed to be oblivious to anything going on, I had now come to understand that the reason for bringing me to church was linked to the belief that I was a witch and that ruined the church experience for me.

REFLECTIVE QUESTION

What are your thoughts regarding the new pattern of church attendance adopted by Awura Adjoa's parents?

One weekend, things changed at home even more for me when I was told I would be going to stay with my step-grandmother (my stepmother's mother) and attend school from there. My parents explained the reason as being due to my school being closer to her house than ours. I was aware that she also had been told by my stepmother that the pastor had confirmed that I was a witch, but I hoped my time living with her would be better and happier. My parents and siblings would visit and my step-grandmother would update my parents on how I was doing. She would often ask me if I was a witch and then sometimes even call me a witch. She used to call me 'small witch' in my African language. I had become used to being called that in my home and within the family. I had also become used to the embarrassment that the label brought me and the pain it caused me inside. I had become used to the mockery and how everything I did, people found a reason to link it or associate it to witchcraft. Clearly my step-grandmother had formed a view on this and had also started to isolate me. I really could not believe what was happening, after all I was just a girl, not a witch.

 Analysis

The United Nations has recognised that being accused of witchcraft is one of the fastest growing issues affecting children in many countries, particularly developing nations such as Nigeria, Gambia, Congo, Guinea and Tanzania (Alston, 2009). However, there continues to be a lack of certainty about the scale of this issue in developed countries.

Research suggests that once a person is labelled a 'witch', they become ostracised from the family and community and people are told to actively avoid the witch. In addition *'children are less able to repel from physical assault by their much larger and physically stronger adversaries'* (Adinkrah, 2011, p 750). Labels of witchcraft result in the legitimisation of abuse towards the victim (Chaudhury, 2012), as was the case in this narrative.

Awura Adjoa's experience of being labelled a witch came at a cost, the cost of her being moved to live with yet another relative. Again, it is clear this step-grandmother was not a blood relation; however, the reasons for her move must have been discussed with her step-grandmother and she had formed an opinion about Awura Adjoa and was already calling her *small witch*, a label which Awura Adjoa had hoped would not follow her to this new home.

The rationale given to Awura Adjoa was around distance to school; however, this ought to have been an earlier consideration before the choice of school was made. It also appears that Awura Adjoa was not consulted about the decision for her to live with her step-grandmother. One cannot help but notice the pattern of non-consultation and non-participation in decisions which invariably affected Awura Adjoa.

Labelling, according to Cunningham and Cunningham (2008), refers to titles or tags which are evocative, largely negative and given to individuals or groups of people. Having been labelled a *witch* and in some instances a *small witch*, Awura Adjoa was then subjected to maltreatment which correlated with the label. As a consequence of the label, Obadina (2012) suggests that once children are accused and labelled as witches, they face exorcism and are confined either to their homes or churches, where various practices take place which are believed to be the solution to ridding them of their evil possession.

It is the view of Bernard and Gupta (2008) that many parents of African origin living in Britain undertake work which is usually low pay, resulting in them undertaking multiple jobs or working for long hours. Awura Adjoa's father appeared to work such long hours and although it is unclear about the exact nature of his employment, this meant that he was rarely at home to observe Awura Adjoa for himself and to form an opinion about her. His absence also meant that he could not be witness to some of the behaviours and utterances made by Awura Adjoa's stepmother. It is acknowledged that on his return from work he would ask Awura Adjoa about her day and verify what he had been told by his wife; however, it remained the case that he appeared to have 'heard' Awura Adjoa but not listened. A case in point is when they returned from the exorcism/church service and he took an open Bible to Awura Adjoa to place under her pillow. This action reinforced the stepmother's and the pastor's declarations and pronouncements.

Doyle and Timms (2014) have suggested that in situations where one child is the target of abuse and scapegoating over the others, it is important that any assessment includes a comprehensive and thorough understanding of the family dynamics, relationships and responsibilities. This will shed some light on any patterns of concern arising from the '*Cinderella syndrome*' (p 83) where a birth child is being favoured over a step-child, for example.

FEELINGS AND LEARNING CHECK

Consider how the narrative contained in this chapter has made you feel.

Reflect on what you knew before and what you have learned from this chapter.

CHAPTER SUMMARY

It is worth noting that this chapter is particularly lengthy and provides us with further insight into Awura Adjoa's experiences within the church and home. Awura Adjoa is taken to see a pastor in a church who confirms her parents' belief that she is a witch. In church, the pastor and Awura Adjoa's parents form what is described as a circle around her and pray loudly with their hands stretched out over her. This is followed by her father giving her an open Bible to place under her pillow while she slept. Awura Adjoa is taken to midweek church services with a different pastor and subsequently experiences another transition to live with her step-grandmother while her siblings continued to live with their parents. The chapter concludes with Awura Adjoa being called *small witch* by her step-grandmother.

FURTHER READING

Bernard, C and Gupta, A (2008) Black African Children and the Child Protection System. British Journal of Social Work, 38: 476–92.

Obadina, S (2012) Witchcraft Accusations and Exorcisms: A Form of Child Abuse. British Journal of School Nursing, 7(6): pp 287–91.

6 You don't belong here, go home

Life after being accused, labelled and tainted as a witch was different to the adventurous life I was excited about when I first heard I would be coming to the UK. The label had not only cost me affection from my parents, but also cost me my confidence and happiness as a child. I had looked forward to coming to live with my parents, and irrespective of the later revelation that my mother as I knew her from the start was actually my stepmother, I still hoped to have a better life and experience in the UK. Sadly, those hopes and dreams were no longer in sight and at this stage, I had been indirectly evicted from my parents' home, and my step-grandmother's home was the only place I appeared to have been accepted into.

REFLECTIVE QUESTIONS

What is your view about the change to the living arrangements for Awura Adjoa?

In your opinion, should Awura Adjoa have been consulted about her views with regards to living with her step-grandmother? Why?

Staying with my step-grandmother was in itself not a positive experience. Among the many accusations she made about me being a witch, she also refrained from allowing me to help her with certain things around the house. My step-grandmother's home also became the place where family meetings about me would take place and during these meetings, I was made to feel like I did not belong in the family. The extent to which my step-grandmother had believed I was a witch became clear to me when one day after being insulted and called a witch, I had cried so much that I felt physically ill, and this continued until I began to throw up. My step-grandmother and my stepmother quickly grabbed a bucket for me to throw up in. As I threw up my step-grandmother took a video recorder which they used to record me as I vomited. I was in tears, I felt sick to my stomach, and I was burning up with a temperature, and instead of my health being a concern to them, they were instead making a recording of me. As a child, I seldom became ill and from the time I arrived from West Africa I had only experienced headaches (on and off) and had visited the GP twice. The first visit to the GP was for a standard check-up and to be registered and the second visit to the GP was after I had cried myself to sleep on many occasions. I recall that even during these visits to the GP, my father would do all the talking and the doctor would barely speak to me.

REFLECTIVE QUESTIONS

In your opinion, should the GP have directly questioned and spoken to Awura Adjoa? What are your reasons for this view?

What effect do you think the GP's approach would have had on Awura Adjoa?

I would just sit with my father holding onto me as the GP checked me over and afterwards he provided a prescription. Vomiting on this day and being recorded had made me so embarrassed and I found it strange that no one seemed to have been concerned about my health.

REFLECTIVE QUESTIONS

How would you have responded to Awura Adjoa being sick in the way described above?

What sense do you make of the response she received from her stepmother and step-grandmother?

THE VOMITING EVENT

© Harry Venning

That evening, on his way home from work, my father passed by my step-grandmother's house to pick up my stepmother and they both showed him the vomit which was in the bucket and also the recording of me throwing up. Then in my native language, my stepmother said that this was the witchcraft that I was vomiting out. I looked at her in disbelief. I was ill and here she was finding a link between my vomiting and being a witch, which she believed I was. My father did not say anything to me and I was asked to go upstairs to my room. The experience of isolation and segregation worsened at my step-grandmother's when, at the age of 11, she said I had to cook for myself and that because I was a witch, I should know how to cook and look after myself. She went ahead to give me a cooking pot, a plate, drinking glass, a tea cup and cutlery while making it clear to me that these were my utensils and that I was not to use or share the same utensils as everyone else ever again. She said she did not want me transferring my witchcraft to the plates and cups in the house and that was why she had given me my own set to use.

REFLECTIVE QUESTIONS

In your opinion, is 11 years old an appropriate age for a child to be cooking and taking care of themselves?

How similar or different is this from that of a young carer?

I had experienced enough shame, pain and isolation that even though I knew I was not a witch, I began to hate myself and think of myself as evil. At school, I continued to be quiet, and tried very hard not to tell anyone about what was going on at home. I thought to myself that some of the aunties and uncles knew what was going on at home but did nothing to help me, and so how on earth could a teacher at school help me? I saw no way they could help, and so even when I came close to deciding to tell someone at school, I held back. There were days where I wished there was someone I could tell who would believe me and take me away from home. But then where to? Who would look after me? I was in no condition to look after myself at that age.

REFLECTIVE QUESTIONS

Drawing upon your understanding of human behaviour, in what ways do you feel that Awura Adjoa's self-perception may have been damaging?

How might teachers and other school-based staff encourage and empower children and young people to discuss their concerns?

Telling someone at church was out of the question because I believed that a pastor belonging to a church, although not my regular church, was the reason why things had deteriorated at home. So for me, it was not an option at any point to tell any of the aunties or uncles at church.

I cherished the daily walk to and from school. It allowed me space to be alone in my thoughts. At school, I would stay in the toilet during break times because I thought I was evil, as that was what I was being told at home. I didn't want to cause harm or inflict evil onto anyone so I tried as much as possible to keep to myself at school. I felt like I didn't belong anywhere. I didn't belong at home because according to them I was a witch. I didn't belong in church because a pastor had contributed to my current circumstances. And I didn't belong in school because, well, there was nothing school could do, at least that is what I thought at the time.

 Analysis

Awura Adjoa began to experience extreme forms of isolation while her stepmother and step-grandmother continued to spread rumours that she was a witch. Gershman (2015) has confirmed that isolation and a breakdown in relationship often occurs between family members and the person accused of being a witch. Of particular relevance was the incident during which Awura Adjoa had become physically unwell and due to violent sobbing she had started to throw up. Surprisingly, the response to her being sick was to video record it and collect it into a bucket as some kind of evidence of witchcraft and to show it to her father.

Awura Adjoa's step-grandmother, as part of the isolation and exclusion, had identified specific cooking pots, cutlery and plates for Awura Adjoa to use and to store in a specific place. This separation of utensils in addition to asking Awura Adjoa to cook her own meals was perhaps a step too far in the wrong direction and reinforced their belief that she was a witch.

At 11 years of age, children in the UK would not be expected to cook full hot meals for themselves; therefore, this strategy was also potentially contributing to the gender bias, which according to Dominelli and McLeod (1989) illuminates the oppressive realities for many women and girls.

According to Moore (2008), contemporary research on stepfamilies has found that a biological tie to children has greater influence on adult involvement in childrearing than gender.

It has been suggested by Nzira (2011) that one of the roles of grandparents within African communities is to settle disputes and officiate during important family events and occasions. The image of Awura Adjoa's step-grandmother appears to be in conflict with the role proposed by Nzira.

If anything, Awura Adjoa's step-grandmother appeared to perpetuate the abuse and ill-treatment Awura Adjoa was receiving and she did this through her actions (calling her a witch and giving her her own set of utensils and crockery) and by omission (declining to cook for Awura Adjoa). This therefore highlights the need for social workers to be cautious of their constructions of grandparents and the grandparenting role, particularly within the context of African families. Pitcher and Arnill (2010) argue that there is an unclear and often uncertain role for grandparents as they negotiate the complexity involved in '*supporting their own adult children in their parenting*' (p 19) and this will be examined in further detail in Chapter 10.

The emotional and psychological impact of labelling Awura Adjoa a witch clearly contributed to her inability to form and maintain friendships at school and to relate to other children within her age and year group. Consequently, the loneliness and isolation was not only experienced within the home environment but had also found its way to school where the impact resulted in Awura Adjoa spending break and lunch times on her own in the toilet in a bid to keep away from everyone. Consistent with an allegation of this nature, the church and its members are more likely at this point to avoid and exclude people who are labelled witches, especially if they have not been exorcised. The contradiction does not escape us as we consider what values many churches purport to uphold within communities. The misconception that churches are always places where hope and tranquillity can be restored is one that requires strict reconsideration, especially as Asamoah-Gyadu (2015) has proposed that witchcraft accusations are reinforced by mostly Christian preachers and preaching.

Awura Adjoa's experiences lead her to conclude that she does not belong, and we are reminded by May (2011) that belonging is a relationship between the self and society. The absence of feeling a sense of belonging meant that Awura Adjoa did not feel a connectedness to her surroundings, despite trying her best to fit in.

One day in school, my classteacher asked me to stay in after one of my lessons. She waited for everyone to leave the classroom and sat down opposite me. She smiled and asked me if I was OK. I forced a fake smile and told her that I was fine. She smiled back. I vividly remember her friendly face. She told me I could talk to her if I ever had a problem in and out of school. She let me go out to play with the other kids and as I left the class, I remember thinking how nice it was of her to sit with me. The school day would soon be over and I would be so afraid to go home. After some time, my classteacher and I had got into a routine of her talking to me before I went out for break and finding out if I was OK. Then one day, she asked me if I was OK and went further to ask how things were at home. Without intending to, tears started rolling down my cheeks. She hugged me and then started to wipe away my tears. I quickly realised I was crying and I told her every-thing was fine. She was not convinced and asked me the reason for the tears. I tried to convince her that everything was fine. She told me she had heard what I'd said and to come back to her if I had any future concerns.

At school, I began to feel grateful that I had her there and I felt she cared. A part of me thought that if I told her what was going on at home, she too might be scared of me and start staying away. However, through her, I was starting to feel a lot happier at school and that was a great feeling. At home, I was the black sheep. I had become used to it. I had accepted it. I had also perfected the art of keeping up appearances unintentionally when we were out as a family. I felt grateful to be living at my step-grandmother's house, because at least I had a place to live.

By this time, I had come to understand and believe that there was something in me that was evil and that I myself was evil. I did not feel I wanted my teachers at school to know what was going on in case they became wary of me too. I didn't know whether they would believe me or understand what I would tell them. I didn't think they would be able to sup-port me.

REFLECTIVE QUESTIONS

What do you make of the teacher's involvement and intervention?

Is there more that could have been done? If so, what; if not, why not?

It was a frequent occurrence at my step-grandmother's that my parents would hold meet-ings with her and if I was home, I would be asked to go upstairs, which I suppose was so that I would not hear what was discussed. This occurred regularly until one evening, just before going to bed, my parents came to my step-grandmother's house. My father called me downstairs and as I stood with my hands behind my back, he asked, 'You are aware of everything that is going on, aren't you?' 'Yes father', I responded. Then he said the words I didn't anticipate and was not prepared to hear: 'You are going back home to West Africa tomorrow. I have bought your ticket and your mother and I will pack your suitcase in preparation for your return.' I felt my legs wanting to give up on me out of fear. Then my father began speaking in my native language. Those words broke my heart and I suddenly realised that he also thought that I was a witch or at the very least believed my stepmother's version of events. My heart started beating very fast. My legs were numb. I went down on my knees and began to plead with my father as tears ran down my cheeks. 'Please father, please don't send me away', was what I blurted out repeatedly. He asked me to stand up and go upstairs to bed. As I stood up, I noticed my stepmother had her head down so I was unable to make eye contact or see her facial expression. I said good-night to both her and my father as well as my step-grandmother and went upstairs to bed. Did I say to bed? Well I went to bed alright, but I most definitely did not sleep.

That night as I lay in bed, I reflected on everything that had happened right from the very beginning: the time I was in West Africa preparing to join my parents; the time I arrived in England; when I first ate grapes; the day I saw my father and he hugged me; the day my stepmother went to school with me to enrol; the day things started to go wrong; the day I was called a witch; the days I was bullied in school for the colour of my skin and where I come from; and then today, the day I was told I was going back to West Africa where I was no longer going to be with my parents. I had endured all this and now this was the outcome? All I did was cry. I wondered whether perhaps my teacher at school had called my parents to find out if everything was OK. After all, she had seen me crying and had asked if everything was OK but I lied and said all was well at home. As I lay down in bed, all I could do was cry and cry some more. I felt the tears leave my eyes, run down my cheeks and into my ears.

That night felt like the shortest night of my life and before I knew it, it was morning. I got up, showered and got dressed, and as I did that, a part of me hoped that things would have changed from the night before but they had not. The decision had been made. I did not belong here any more and I was being sent back to West Africa. My parents arrived that morning to come and take me to the airport. Nothing much was said and I was ready when they arrived; I said goodbye to my step-grandmother who started crying as she said goodbye to me. I was baffled, 'Why was she crying?' I asked myself. I felt her reaction was hypocritical because after all they had all taken part in this decision. I sat in the car and my parents drove me to the airport. After having my bags checked in, it was time to go through security and I had to bid farewell to my parents. My stepmother started crying, begging my father to change his decision, but he was not going back on his words. As tears rolled down my cheeks, I hugged them one at a time and then waved goodbye at them as I walked away and slowly I lost sight of them as I entered the security screening section of the airport with an uncle (chaperone). I went through the departure processes and continued my journey home, back to West Africa.

Analysis

The decision to return Awura Adjoa to West Africa was one which was made without her consent or participation. It is important to consider the role of children and young people in decision-making within the context of the home environment in many ethnic minority families and particularly within families more generally.

Awura Adjoa's father appears to have been pressurised to reach this decision in a bid to maintain what they believed to be peace and tranquillity within the family home. Through this action, he had shown himself to be an adult who was unable to maintain and secure a safe and calm family environment for all his children. Therefore, the selection process in relation to who mattered and who did not, was down to the members of the family and a step-grandmother. Doyle et al (2010, p 239) found that survivors of emotional abuse did not necessarily find their grandparents supportive as they were '*too involved in the family dynamics to be helpful*'.

In addition, it is difficult to consider what the role of the other siblings may have been within this process; however, Doyle and Timms (2014) note that in a similar situation, children who appear to be favoured over their siblings may feel powerless to intervene as confronting or challenging their parents might aggravate the situation further. At this stage, Awura Adjoa was rejected, abandoned, despised and finally returned to West Africa, where she had come from two years earlier. Research by Baumeister (2005) has indicated that the human brain reacts to rejection in the same way as an injury of a physical nature. This is important when considering what the impact that this level of rejection may have had on Awura Adjoa.

FEELINGS AND LEARNING CHECK

Consider how the narrative contained in this chapter has made you feel.

Reflect on what you knew before and what you have learned from this chapter.

CHAPTER SUMMARY

This chapter has highlighted the events leading to Awura Adjoa's enforced return to West Africa. This begins with her being sent to live with her step-grandmother with the reason given that this was nearer her new secondary school. While with her step-grandmother, she is given her own cooking utensils and crockery and told she must cook and care for herself. Her step-grandmother and her mother record Awura Adjoa being sick into a bucket with the intent of using this video recording as evidence of her being a witch. Awura Adjoa explains the renewed interest by one of her teachers in her welfare which comes at the point where Awura Adjoa's father informs her about the decision to return her to West Africa.

FURTHER READING

Akilapa, R and Simkiss, D (2012) Cultural Influences and Safeguarding Children. Paediatrics and Child Health, *22(11): 490–5.*

Cohan, J A (2011) The Problem of Witchcraft Violence in Africa. Suffolk University Law Review, *44(4): 803–72.*

7 In the end

My trip back home was one that felt very lonely, even though I was accompanied by a relative (an uncle) who was going on holiday to West Africa. My parents had asked him to look after me during the journey home. The excitement I felt during my first experience on a plane should have been the same feeling I experienced going back, as I ought to have been looking forward to telling my friends and other family members all about my experiences in the UK. However, what and how I felt was far off from excitement and enthusiasm. Throughout the journey, I was awake and restless. My thoughts were all over the place and while I pondered my fate, I continued to shed more and more tears.

REFLECTIVE QUESTION

What are your views about the travel arrangements made for Awura Adjoa to return to West Africa?

I did not know what to expect going back home; I thought that people in West Africa would have been informed that I was a witch and that would result in me receiving worse treatment, particularly more physical abuse than that which I had experienced in the UK. This thought made me more scared, nervous and frightened of what was to come when I got back home. The most heartbreaking thought was that once again I was going to a life that meant being far away from my parents and living with one relative or another.

REFLECTIVE QUESTION

What could have been done to minimise Awura Adjoa's anxieties about her return to West Africa?

When I arrived in West Africa, I was met at the airport by one of my father's siblings. I had no idea about the arrangements made for me up until that point. The relative I travelled with had been told who would pick me up from the airport so as we stepped out into the waiting area of the airport, he looked through the crowd and recognised my uncle who was picking me up. I did not recognise this uncle who had come to meet me, although he said he knew me as a much younger child. He hugged me and collected my bags from my uncle. They spoke in private for a brief period during which time I began to feel *anxious about what they may have been discussing. We said our goodbyes and I went home with my receiving uncle where I spent the first night.*

The next day, my uncle woke me up and I got ready for the day. I was very quiet and was still in quite a sad mood, trying to make sense of what had taken place over the last few days. Surprisingly, upon waking up in West Africa I felt some weight lifted off me. My uncle treated me with so much love and care and so I had no immediate reason to continue to feel anxious or concerned. I stayed with him for two days and he informed me that my father had given him instructions about my longer-term care before I arrived. I was to live with my aunt, whom again I didn't remember but who apparently knew me from when I was younger. Leaving my uncle, I felt very sad, particularly because I was just getting used to being loved and shown care. Most importantly, he had not called me a witch or ill-treated me.

My uncle took me to my aunt who I was going to be staying with and the reception when I arrived at her home was warm and welcoming. She had a beautiful family and children who were older than me, and meeting them made me feel a lot more comfortable and relieved from the nervousness I had been feeling during the journey to her home. My uncle and my aunt spoke while I played with her children in the communal compound. Life at my aunt's home was pleasant; however, I was still broken by the experience of being labelled a witch in the UK. I was still cautious of how I lived and kept to myself to avoid any similar treatment from my aunt and/or her children.

It was unclear whether or not my aunt and her children believed in witchcraft; however, what was clear was that she had a very different attitude towards me. She was kind, accommodating and caring.

 ## Analysis

The narrative above by Awura Adjoa suggests that she had been excluded from all discussions and planning in relation to her return to West Africa. It bears striking similarity to her experience of travelling to the UK. To this end, Mather and Kerac (2002, p 44) argue that *'the decision to move is often made for children rather than with them. They move from their country of origin to a country of reception, from the familiar to the different, from fitting in to standing out.'*

Awura Adjoa was not sure whether her father had shared any information with others and if he had, what kind of information he had shared. What did he tell the chaperone who travelled with her? That Awura Adjoa cried throughout the journey back evidenced how sad she must have been and raises concern about why her uncle (chaperone) did not appear to be interested or concerned about her overall well-being and mood. On arrival in West Africa, Awura Adjoa is met by an uncle, and after two days is sent to an aunt who Awura Adjoa learns will be her main carer. These are not the same relatives who took care of Awura Adjoa prior to her leaving for the UK; however, Awura Adjoa felt some relief and gratitude about the different and positive attitudes towards her on return.

After many weeks of being back, I was home one day when I saw my father at the gate. I felt my stomach turn. He didn't look happy as he came in and he said hello to me. Following close behind him was my stepmother. 'What were they doing here?' was the question going through my mind. We went inside the house and as per the usual reception given in African households, my aunt offered them something to drink and eat. I stayed out with the other children and we played. The other children were more excited than I was about my parents' presence. Some asked me why I wasn't as excited as them. I brushed off their questions because I was afraid that if I disclosed my experiences to them, they would distance themselves from me in the belief I was a witch.

Not long after, I heard my aunt and my parents busily talking and my father was shouting, saying in our native language that I had come and attempted to ruin the family back in the UK. I overheard him retelling the story about my little sister and me on the window ledge. As I listened to him, I could hear the anger in his voice and that scared me even more. I wanted to run and hide. They called me in after some time and as I stood in front of them, tears started rolling down my cheeks. I looked at my aunt who seemed the only person on my side as tears rolled down her cheeks too. My father asked me the very question I had heard over and over again while in the UK: 'Was I a witch?' And he asked whether I had confessed to anything since I arrived in West Africa. I responded and said 'no' while my chest felt like it was tightening up with every breath I took.

REFLECTIVE QUESTION

What are your views about the arrival of Awura Adjoa's father and stepmother and his line of questioning?

My aunt asked me to go out and continue playing with the other children and so I went out. It seemed the other children had overheard some of what was being said and when I came out, no one said a word, nor was I in the frame of mind to say anything to them. I sat down outside and as I sat waiting, my parents came out. My father asked to take a picture with me and so I cleaned up my face and smiled as my aunt took the picture. Shortly afterwards they said their goodbyes and said they were leaving.

I felt heartbroken about the emotional distance between me and my father in particular. I didn't say much to my stepmother. I went back into the house after they had left and when my aunt returned from seeing them off, she found me in tears. She tried to console me and also told me that the reason why my parents had come back was because a problem had arisen in the UK and that my school in the UK had been asking about my whereabouts. This, apparently, was why they needed to come to take some photographs to evidence that I was safe. I didn't know how true this was, but I began to think about my teacher who had asked me shortly before my departure whether everything was OK with me at home. I thought of the possibility that she may have been interceding for me from a distance; however, I realised it would probably be too late and this thought resulted in more uncontrollable tears.

In the days that followed, I felt like I was a victim of the passing of time, simply stagnant while everybody else appeared to be living happily. I had no interest in any activities and did not want to be in the midst of people. I thought of myself as evil because that was what I had been repeatedly told.

 Analysis

Keeping children safe in safeguarding is everyone's business in the UK; however, from the short time that Awura Adjoa lived in the UK it is clear that a number of circumstances and opportunities were missed to find out and understand how this girl was living. The decision by her school to request evidence of her safety and well-being should be applauded; however, as before, it is unclear what they did with the photograph and indeed to what extent these enquiries were made about her safety and her well-being.

Statutory guidance on safeguarding children in schools is very clear about teachers and other educational staff making prompt and effective referrals or investigations into the safeguarding of children in schools in their care. Anecdotally and also according to Nzira (2011), many African families consider taking their children back to the home country during certain points in their upbringing. This return to the home country might be because of behaviour, family commitments, financial difficulties or other forms of pressure. It is then the case that these children will be under the radar and not heard of until the parents and carers decide to return them to the UK.

Clearly, at that point, Awura Adjoa was not a British citizen but she was a child in need of protection and care like any other child in the UK. The *Working Together to Safeguard Children* (DfE, 2015) document makes it absolutely clear that where there is a concern about the health and well-being and safety of a child that this must be made known and shared with relevant agencies. It is heartwarming to find that such legislation and policy acknowledges, supports and protects all children in the UK, including children who may be from ethnic minority backgrounds and who may not hold British citizenship.

There was no indication about whether or not links were made between Awura Adjoa's behaviour while at school and her current absence from school. It remains unclear what the school authorities were told by her parents; however, we must be cautious not to jump to conclusions about deceit, fraud or indeed blatant lying. It is not irrational to assume that once a child is missing from school and where there have been previous concerns (documented or not) to take into account, the whereabouts of a child becomes a subject for interrogation. It can be assumed that the school authorities indeed progressed their investigations about the whereabouts of Awura Adjoa and this is what possibly led to her parents returning to West Africa to take photographic evidence about her well-being and welfare. Therein lies the gap in practice and the gap in safeguarding vulnerable children who may also have a home outside of the UK. Is photographic evidence sufficient?

Broadhurst et al (2005) in their study about children who are missing from school concluded that schools play a central role in child safeguarding and that it is important to understand the processes and systems that are in place to monitor, record and act on situations where children are missing from school. Their research identified the factors which provided fertile ground for disengagement with education. These were: lone parent families, experience of domestic violence, history of mental health difficulties, divorce and separation, poor housing conditions, a dependence on state benefits and at least one child with a disability, emotional and behavioural difficulties (p 109). It is difficult to draw conclusions on the ethnicity of any of the participants as this was not addressed in the study; however, it may be possible to surmise the inclusion of some ethnic minority families within the sample, especially as it was drawn from a number of local education authorities in London, which has an increasing number of black and ethnic minority children in its schools. The point being made here is that there is perhaps still the need for research to be conducted into the specific experiences of black minority ethnic children who are missing from education.

This corroborates the view put forward by Bernard and Gupta (2008), who refer to a period in 2001 where over 300 boys between the ages of four and seven were identified to have gone missing from schools in the London area. With the exception of one child, all the others were of black African origin and were thought to have been returned to Africa.

Botham (2011) also found that children became 'invisible' when they were not in education and that this invisibility would make such children more susceptible to trafficking, forced and early marriage, unsafe care and lack of protection.

Weeks after being back in West Africa my aunt told me we were going to go to see someone she knew who would help me enrol into school. When we arrived there, I found out that this person was a proprietor of the school as well as a pastor of a church. My aunt introduced me to him and with a smile on his face he hugged me and said in our native tongue, 'Welcome'. He spoke to my aunt while I sat in a corner of the room scared to the bottom of my stomach. I started to have flashbacks; I felt I was breaking into a sweat as I replayed over and over again in my head the time when I was taken to the pastor in the UK by my parents and how he had told them I was a witch. I was frightened. Was this man about to tell my aunt I was a witch? Was she pretending when she was nice to me and only a few weeks later was trying to confirm whether I was a witch?

After a while of them talking, my aunt called me to come to them and then the man asked us to pray. As he prayed, I prepared myself for the worst. Following my experience in the UK, I was certain he too was about to ruin things for me and accuse me of being a witch. When he finished praying, he smiled at me and said that he was looking forward to seeing me at school. He then turned to my aunt and said in our native language that I was not a witch. My aunt turned and looked at me and smiled. I acted oblivious to what was going on but in my heart, I felt such joy knowing that this man, whose words I knew would be taken very seriously, had vindicated me. We went home and thereafter life was filled with me returning to my old self, the happy girl I once was.

REFLECTIVE QUESTIONS

What are your thoughts about Awura Adjoa's experience of this pastor in West Africa?

How do you think the pastor's conclusion may have impacted on Awura Adjoa's welfare?

Life's difficulties were inevitable, but I felt I could now live without being overshadowed by the label 'witch' and being subjected to treatment which threatened my safety, security and my life as a whole. It has taken a lot of time since then to pull myself back up. Other tragic and more difficult experiences have come my way after the accusation of being a witch, but it is clear to me that those things happened after I had been a victim of child witchcraft abuse. Over time I transformed back to the happy child I once was, embracing the culture I love so much and believing that I am a good person with so much to give. The very faith and beliefs that were used against me which contributed to me being labelled a witch were also the very faith and beliefs that helped me through my recovery from all that I had been through.

I am unashamedly Christian and my relationship with God has increasingly become stronger. With time, I came to realise that some people hide behind religion and beliefs to cause pain and trauma to others.

My dreadful and unfortunate experience of witchcraft labelling and abuse seemed to have been very quickly forgotten and no one ever mentioned it again. After four years of being back in West Africa, my parents had started to hint about me returning to the UK; however, I was not particularly keen to do so due to my childhood experiences. It was as though it never happened as no one ever made reference to it. However, four years later when I was nearly 16, older and wiser, I accepted the invitation to return to join my parents and siblings in the UK. This time my parents came to Africa to sort out my documents and accompanied me on the trip. Over time, with the help of new friendships I formed, particularly in school, I was able to settle back into the UK.

My experiences of child witchcraft abuse and my survival and recovery has only made me stronger. I have chosen to share my story so that I can become helpful to vulnerable children. Today I am a university graduate and a young woman with a big heart, with a desire to challenge cultural and religious beliefs and practices which put the safety and well-being of a person at risk. At the centre of my heart is a heavy passion for child safeguarding because while I survived, I am aware that today, there are many children who have or are experiencing either similar or worse experiences to mine and who just like me are afraid to speak up. Just like me, I know they are unaware that the school can actually do something to help, that a neighbour could help or that the GP could help. I refuse to allow this experience to hold me back and while the scars remain in my heart and memory, I endeavour to hold up the banner to fight against child witchcraft abuse so that children's lives will be better safeguarded and their future better secured. I hope that each time I stand as an ambassador of child protection the little girl who once suffered will be atoned for the pain and suffering she went through as just a girl and not a witch.

Analysis

Awura Adjoa was sent back to West Africa, corroborating the conclusion by Bahunga (2013) that children accused of being *witches* in the UK may be sent overseas to family members. The remit and duties of these family members differ within families; however, it is clear that for some, the duty will be to organise and arrange an exorcism or persecute the child into a confession.

Back in Africa, children are dispatched to a wide variety of settings. Some stay with a relative and enrol in whichever school other children in the family attend (Bledsoe and Sow, 2011), and this appeared to be the case with Awura Adjoa who was enrolled into a school which was familiar to her aunt. Interestingly, Awura Adjoa was not given any reports or correspondence from her school in the UK to inform the decision about which year/stage or level she would be enrolled into.

Peng and Wong (2016) have suggested that there is often not a wide pool of willing caregivers to choose from when decisions are being made as to who will look after the child/children in the absence of their parents. In the case of Awura Adjoa, we know that she was not consulted about the impending return, nor did she have a choice about who she would be returning to.

Little consideration was given to the fact that Awura Adjoa was now back in Africa on her own without her parents and without her siblings. What she perceived as a reunion with her parents and siblings was shortlived and there appeared to be no further discussion about her birth mother or the impact of the disclosure in relation to her birth mother.

Kline et al (2008, p 295) reported that experiences such as Awura Adjoa's often resulted in a '*distant and conflicted relationship with church leaders and a stronger relationship with God*'. This is what Awura Adjoa describes towards the end of her narrative when she says that faith helped her to work through her experiences.

FEELINGS AND LEARNING CHECK

Consider how the narrative contained in this chapter has made you feel.

Reflect on what you knew before and what you have learned from this chapter.

CHAPTER SUMMARY

This chapter has addressed the difficult return of Awura Adjoa to West Africa. She returns with a chaperone and initially is met at the airport by an uncle who takes her to her aunt with whom Awura Adjoa will live with on a more permanent basis. Awura Adjoa acknowledges that she is happy living with her aunt, who has children, and arrangements are made for her to be taken to another pastor who concludes that she is not a witch. She is enrolled into school and hopes to be able to put her experiences in the UK behind her.

Weeks later her parents arrive in the country, presumably because her school in the UK had been enquiring about her whereabouts. They start off quite angry, asking whether or not Awura Adjoa had confessed to being a witch while in West Africa. It is unclear whether Awura Adjoa's aunt informs them of the conclusions from the pastor in West Africa about her not being a witch; however, there is little evidence of remorse on the part of her parents for sending her to West Africa. Instead, they took photographs of her and left, returning to the UK with photographs they could show to school authorities as evidence that Awura Adjoa was safe and well.

FURTHER READING

Botham, J (2011) *The Complexities of Children Missing from Education: A Local Project to Address the Health Needs of School-aged Children.* Community Practitioner, *84(5): 31–4.*

Department for Education (DfE) (2016) Children Missing Education: Statutory Guidance for Local Authorities. *London: HMSO.*

Part 2 Implications for practice

Theoretical reflections

This chapter will consider the cycle of witchcraft abuse, adapted from Cimpric (2010), and which reflects the experience of Awura Adjoa. This will be followed by an examination of relevant policy, legislative frameworks and theoretical perspectives. According to Cimpric (2010), victims of witchcraft accusations go through a cycle, often beginning with a problem or issue for which there appears to be no explanation for or solution to. In the case of a child, they are scapegoated and blamed as possessing witchcraft (usually by a well-respected person within the faith community). They are then taken for exorcism and the cycle starts again when a different problem or issue arises.

Figure 8.1 clearly depicts the cycle through which Awura Adjoa progressed in her experience. She was sleeping in the daytime, bedwetting at night and was forgetful. These incidents were ongoing and resulted in her being ignored and isolated from her parents, wider family and siblings. Following a period of isolation, Awura Adjoa was taken to meet a pastor in church who declared Awura Adjoa to be a witch. The process of exorcism took place and they returned home; however, after a short period of time, Awura Adjoa was removed from the family home and sent to live with her step-grandmother where she was further isolated and continued to be accused. As she was parented from a distance, her father and stepmother visited regularly to find out how Awura Adjoa was doing and she continued to go to school from the home of her step-grandmother.

Finally, Awura Adjoa was sent back to West Africa.

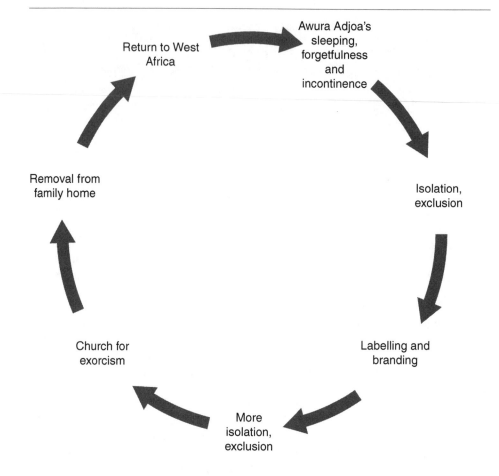

Figure 8.1   Cycle of witchcraft abuse (adapted from Cimpric, 2010)

POLICY, PRACTICE GUIDANCE AND LAW

In this section, we review the range of policy and legislative frameworks which currently underpin social work intervention and which could be used to work with families where witchcraft labelling has occurred and children are at risk of harm.

The preamble for the United Nations Convention on the Rights of the Child (UNCRC) requires that we '*recognise the child, for the full and harmonious development of his or her personality, should grow up in a family environment in an atmosphere of happiness, love and understanding*' (UN Convention on the Rights of the Child, 1990).

Children have the right to live in safe and secure homes without abuse, harm and mal-treatment. Their rights under the UNCRC give children an entitlement to leisure, recrea-tion and play as well as the right to participate in matters concerning them. It is interesting when considering these rights for children that Awura Adjoa appeared not to have any time for play and recreation, a situation which she initially used as a strategy to keep away from trouble. In the UK, her label of *witch* placed her in a situation where she was unable to play with her peers due to the stigma and her self-doubt. Roose and De Bie (2008) have suggested that children's rights should not be concerned with which rights children actually have but rather how these rights might be realised. Consequently, we implore social workers to consider ways in which they might support children like Awura Adjoa to experience and achieve their rights.

The Every Child Matters (ECM) agenda popularised after the death of Victoria Climbié and given legal backing by the Children Act 2004 emphasised the requirement for all children to meet five key outcomes: stay safe; enjoy and achieve; be healthy; make a positive contribution; and achieve economic well-being (DfES, 2004). Despite being minimally used in contemporary social work practice, ECM provides a useful framework through which the well-being of all children can remain the focus of interventions.

With regard to Awura Adjoa's case of witchcraft labelling, we invite you to consider where and how her experiences achieved or were at odds with the essence of ECM.

Be healthy
Stay safe
Enjoy and achieve
Make a positive contribution
Achieve economic well-being

Working Together to Safeguard Children (2015)

This statutory guidance provides detail about the ways in which various professionals should work together to ensure the safety and protection of all children. The guidance makes a firm and renewed commitment to keeping children safe using child-centred approaches and processes which ensure that children are respected and their voices heard. The guidance makes it clear that promoting the welfare of children includes preventing impairment of their development or health; acting to ensure that all children have the best possible outcomes; protecting children from all forms of maltreatment and ensuring that children grow up in secure environments which are safe and effective.

The guidance reiterates the value of early help for families when problems are emerging. This requires proactive responses by social workers and other childcare practitioners.

Safeguarding Children from Abuse Linked to a Belief in Spirit Possession (2007)

This guidance is non-statutory in nature and provides guidance for practitioners who may come into contact with children and young people who may be at risk of this form of abuse. It draws upon principles of good practice in child safeguarding and provides definitions for key terminology linked to this form of abuse. Importantly, this guidance offers some strategies for working with communities and faith leaders to raise awareness on how they might share their concerns about children at risk.

The Children Act 1989

Section 17 – Children in Need

Section 17 of the Children Act 1989 requires the local authority to assess and support children who are deemed to be 'in need'. Children are deemed to be 'in need' when they require services from the local authority to maintain reasonable health and well-being. For example, Awura Adjoa could have been supported as a child in need until a fuller assessment of her needs had been undertaken regarding her fatigue, tears and anxiety.

Section 41, Schedule 8 – Privately fostered children

While in the care of her step-grandmother, it could be argued that Awura Adjoa was in a private fostering arrangement which the local authority needed to be aware of and where necessary ensure an assessment is undertaken of the home. The provisions clearly state that aunts, uncles or grandparents who are fully or partially related by blood cannot be private foster carers. Awura Adjoa's case is unique in that she is not 'blood' related to her stepmother's mother (step-grandmother) and so at the very least the local authority should be able to advise in such unique cases and situations.

Section 44 – Emergency Protection Order (EPO)

This could have benefitted Awura Adjoa if her immediate protection from significant harm was required. This could be used, for example, if social workers were being prevented from access to Awura Adjoa for the purposes of further assessment.

Section 47 – Child Protection Enquiry

Enquiries under Section 47 are undertaken when a child is at risk of significant harm. There is a duty on the local authority to investigate and take necessary steps to ensure a child is safe. In the case of Awura Adjoa, this could have occurred at different points in her narrative 1) through a school referral and subsequent investigation and assessment; 2) through her step-grandmother; 3) through the church and pastor; 4) though other extended family members.

The Children Act 2004

This legislation came into force following the tragic death of Victoria Climbié. Its provisions created the Children's Commissioner and also strengthened the process around ˙˙ fostering.

, it created the duty of the local authority to promote the health and well-being ˈ in their area. Well-being is used within this legislation to mean emotional, and mental health, education, recreation and leisure.

Education Act 1996

If this kind of situation were to arise now, the local education authority would have a duty to investigate the whereabouts of a child before their name can be taken off the school register. The Department for Education (2016b) set out statutory guidance for local authorities, under section 436A of the Education Act 1996 to make arrangements to identify, as far as it is possible to do so, children missing education (CME). Laming (2003) recommended that professionals who work in frontline services, including social workers, ensure that basic information such as the child's name, primary carer, name of the child's school etc must be recorded and updated regularly to ensure children do not become invisible to authorities and statutory services. CME are said to be at significant risk of underachievement, radicalisation or exploitation. The guidance requires parents to satisfy the local authority that their child who has come to the attention of the authorities due to missing education, is actually receiving suitable alternative education.

Human Rights Act 1998 and United Nations Convention on the Rights of the Child

The Human Rights Act 1998 could be considered when working with Awura Adjoa and her family. The right to family life does not only imply living with people who may constitute a family, but also recognises that families should be safe and secure places for children. Article 3, which is the prohibition of torture, inhuman and degrading treatment could be applied to Awura Adjoa in terms of the treatment she received. Article 5, the right to freedom and security, again was not always evident in the narratives provided by Awura Adjoa in that she was taken to live with her step grandmother where her freedom to be a child was compromised. Finally, Article 14 of the Human Rights Act 1998 prohibits all forms of discrimination. It could be argued that Awura Adjoa was discriminated against through her experience of being a step-daughter and being scapegoated and labelled. The UNCRC, which came into being in 1989, represents the United Nations' attempt to bring children's rights under a global umbrella. The UK is a signatory to this international convention, as are ALL the countries in West Africa and this makes it all the more relevant to the experiences of Awura Adjoa. A rights-informed approach to safeguarding children at risk of witchcraft labelling has been outlined in Tedam (2014, pp 9–10).

RELEVANT THEORIES

Theoretically, a number of perspectives could be drawn upon to make sense of this narrative; however, it is considered that the following may be sufficient and relevant to the narrative as it stands:

- family systems theory;
- attachment theory;
- stigma and labelling theory;
- human development theories;
- Maslow's hierarchy of needs;
- gender considerations.

Family systems theory

Family systems theory has emerged from general systems theory and recognises that subsystems within the family are interdependent. This interdependence means that behaviour and emotion from a family member (subsystem) can influence the functioning of other family members (Moore and Buehler, 2011).

Walker (2012) suggests that family dynamics are constantly being altered due to the changes in circumstances of its members. It is important that social workers in particular understand that a family cannot be understood by claiming to understand its single, individual members. Instead, a holistic approach needs to be taken and a critical understanding is needed of the family structure and how it is organised. Awura Adjoa's experiences at home of physical and emotional abuse as well as neglect within her family resulted in her often falling asleep during class and being tearful the majority of the time. The situation was further compounded by the family structure, which included a step-grandmother whose opinion appeared to be highly regarded and whose home children could be sent to when they were no longer welcome in the family home. Family systems theory recognises the importance of family members and their attitudes and behaviours because it can assist a social worker to capture what is acceptable within a family and what is abhorred (Walker, 2012).

Lamb (1986) suggests that there are three types of involvement from parents: accessibility, interaction and responsibility. These, it is argued, will vary from family to family and from culture to culture.

We made a conscious decision to exclude Awura Adjoa's siblings from this narrative for reasons of anonymity; however, it is important to consider the role of her siblings during the time Awura Adjoa was experiencing witchcraft labelling. Questions that practitioners might wish to reflect on in relation to the wider family system include:

- How much did Awura Adjoa's siblings know about the allegation of witchcraft and subsequent labelling?
- How did they feel about the differential treatment experienced within their home? For example, Awura Adjoa going to midweek church service and living with her step-grandmother (who happened to be their biological grandmother).
- Did they feel able to question or challenge their parents about what was happening?
- What were their views about the concept of witchcraft?
- What reason(s) were given to them about why Awura Adjoa was returning to West Africa?

Attachment theory

This is significant in the analysis of Awura Adjoa's experiences because she begins her life being looked after by relatives, thousands of miles away from her parents. The death of her mother when she was a baby and the absence of her father meant that she had to be cared for by others. While this in itself is not necessarily problematic, it does mean that the age at which Awura Adjoa joined her father and the rest of her family was particularly crucial and delicate. Bowlby (1969) argued that separation, even as brief as one week, between mother and child could have a negative impact on the attachment relationship and that it was important for caregivers to be accessible and present for attachment to be formed. Added to this is the fact that the person who Awura Adjoa had always known to be her mother was actually her stepmother. Secure attachment contributes to the healthy development of children and increases the likelihood of a positive self-image and identity. According to Ainsworth (1979), children with secure attachment are able to manage stressful situations by recalling the reassurances and positive strategies received from their mother.

Attachment is a two-way process and so while Awura Adjoa may not have formed a secure attachment to her parents, it would appear her parents were not as secure in their relating to her, something which Bowlby (1969) stated was not uncommon. Awura Adjoa's parents perhaps should have spent time developing their relationship with her from the outset and from the time she arrived in the UK to join them.

Stigma and labelling theory

The original proponent of labelling theory, Howard S Becker, concluded that powerful social actors label behaviour or action as deviant and that these labels then affirm their identity (Becker, 1991).

Goffman (1963, p 3) referred to stigma as a *'deeply discrediting attribute'* while Link and Phelan (2001) add that stigma is a tag that others may attach to a person. Stigma has been said to have negative effects on self-perception, resulting in people feeling less confident and avoidant of social interaction for fear of rejection and further isolation. Four components of stigma have been proposed by Link and Phelan (2001) and these are: labelling, stereotyping, cognitive separation and emotional reactions. Later however, a fifth component of status loss was added by Link et al (2004). The evidence so far suggests that Awura Adjoa experienced stigma through the processes already mentioned: first she was labelled a *witch*, then the stereotypes associated with witchcraft were frequently referred to (for example, when her stepmother asked her to stay awake because she believed that Awura Adjoa would use her witchcraft at night). Awura Adjoa began to internalise what she was being told about herself and started to react emotionally to the labels and stereotypes by crying, being sad and isolating herself, to mention just a few. Finally, Awura Adjoa experienced a loss of her status as a child, step-grandchild and sibling, arising from the behaviours and attitudes towards her. Furthermore, her role as a pupil in school was compromised as she had disengaged with her studies, her peers and her teachers. It is further argued that stigma is created and maintained by structures of power and we see this through the behaviours of Awura Adjoa's parents, her step-grandmother, the pastor and other family members who used their positions of power to further ostracise and stigmatise Awura Adjoa. *'Cultural stigma'*, according to Akilapa and Simkiss (2012, p 492), can result in children from black and other ethnic minority communities being particularly vulnerable to various forms of abuse and maltreatment. It can also lead to isolation and exclusion.

Human development theory

Human growth and development form a crucial part of this narrative, especially in relation to child development. There are many perspectives on human growth and development; however, Erikson's stages of psychosocial development appears to be relevant to Awura Adjoa.

Erikson (1995) expressed the view that human beings grow and develop through a number of stages: trust vs mistrust; autonomy vs shame and doubt; initiative vs guilt; industry vs inferiority; identity vs role confusion; intimacy vs isolation; generativity vs stagnation; integrity vs despair. He argued that children at each stage require support to manage their internal conflicts, otherwise there is an increased likelihood of becoming damaged in adulthood.

Awura Adjoa arrived in Britain aged ten and so could be said to have been in the industry vs inferiority stage of her development where school played a major part in her life. This stage involves children developing socially and they should be able to relate to their peers. If, however, children in this age range hold feelings of inadequacy, they may lose confidence and self-esteem. Trying to understand Awura Adjoa using this stage of Erikson's cycle (1995), we acknowledge that finding out about her birth mother when she did, and with little consideration of helping her work through this loss, would very likely impact on the next stage of identity and role confusion.

Robinson (2007) sheds some insight into theories of human development from a non-Western perspective. She talks about cross-cultural perspectives on attachment theory, identity development, cognitive development, communication and the influence of racial and cultural factors on socialisation. Robinson (2007) explores the concept of *socialisation* and critiques the application of Baumrind's parenting styles to non-white families. She argues that Baumrind's parenting styles '*would not be adequate conceptualisations because they are specific to European-American culture*' (Robinson, 2007, p 141). We agree that approaches to discipline in terms of child-rearing practices are related to the goals and values of socialisation and that parenting styles vary depending on the cultural backgrounds and values of families. These values are described as *individualism* and *collectivism* and Awura Adjoa's parents' deference to collectivism may have in part contributed to the way in which the responsibility for her care and well-being was delegated to others.

Maslow's hierarchy of needs

In 1970, Maslow concluded that all human beings, regardless of their culture, have five basic needs and that children of all backgrounds, nationalities and ethnicities have the same basic human needs. It is beyond the scope of this book to fully interrogate Maslow's theory, offering the challenges and strengths of this framework. However, it is an important consideration for social work practitioners who might come into contact with children who have been labelled witches or who are at risk of this form of abuse.

Maslow's hierarchy of needs, depicted below, begins from the bottom with physiological needs such as air, food, shelter, sleep, excretion and sex.

It would appear that Awura Adjoa's needs across all five levels of the hierarchy were severely compromised.

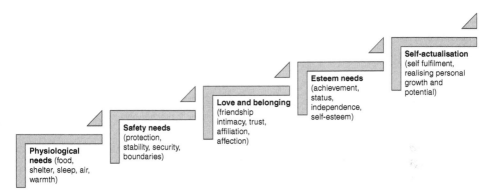

Figure 8.2   Adapted from Maslow's hierarchy of needs (1970)

On the first rung of the hierarchy is the need for clothing, food, shelter, air and sleep. We know that Awura Adjoa lived in a house with her extended family in West Africa and again in the UK. While there was no mention of a lack of food, except for periods where she was encouraged to fast (abstain from food), what was clear was the poor sleep she experienced as a result of the distress she felt. Awura Adjoa appeared to have been deprived of sleep when on a number of occasions she was actively prevented from falling asleep as her stepmother believed that she was an active witch during the night. Awura Adjoa's lack of sleep impacted on her engagement in school and this was noticed by the teachers. She also appeared to be emotionally starved of warmth and love when she was ignored, marginalised and isolated (Doyle and Timms, 2014).

The next rung consists of the need for safety and security, morality, family, health and property. We already know that Awura Adjoa's safety and security were compromised on a regular basis. For example, when she was taken to the pastor who attempted to perform some sort of exorcism on her; when she was being sick and her stepmother and step-grandmother were making a recording of this rather than being concerned about her health, for example.

The third rung on Maslow's hierarchy is the need for love and belonging, family, friendship and sexual intimacy. It does not appear that Awura Adjoa belonged to the family while in the UK. It is also worth noting that within her narrative, she does not once suggest that she felt loved or indeed part of the family. She makes clear reference to the bond with her father; however, this is short-lived as her father becomes a part of the decision for her to return to West Africa. There were also instances where her parents failed to show love; for example, when they sent Awura Adjoa to live with her step-grandmother and when she was singled out to attend midweek church service.

According to Maslow, the fourth rung represents self-esteem, confidence, accomplishment, respect for self and others, all of which we could suggest were not achieved by Awura Adjoa during this period. It is clear that her self-esteem was low the majority of the time. She did not belong and was made to feel that way for a very long time. On one occasion, she had been crying uncontrollably after being accused of attempting to push her sister out of the window. She was ignored by her stepmother and step-grandmother, who appeared to encourage other relatives to do the same. This would contribute to Awura Adjoa having low confidence and self-esteem, particularly as there was an audience of family members, who in her eyes were complicit in the abuse and maltreatment she experienced.

Awura Adjoa recognises that, in terms of Maslow's final rung of self-actualisation, the journey is ongoing and she believes her contribution to this book will go some way in assisting her to develop and enhance her confidence and achieve a level of self-fulfilment.

Gender considerations

Gender considerations are important in social work because they influence the ways in which families function. The practice of witchcraft labelling cuts across gender; however, research suggests that females are more likely than males to be labelled. Research by Adinkrah (2004) and Chaudhury (2012) have supported the view that the majority of witchcraft accusations have been directed towards women. Rodriguez and Henderson (2010), in their study of the link between religiosity and the risk of abusing children in the USA, found that overall females were more likely to physically abuse their children than males. They caution social workers against using this as a predictor of child abuse and instead propose that social workers recognise and acknowledge the relevance of religion and faith in the lives of the families they work with. It is imperative that childcare practitioners review and re-evaluate their engagement with the particular religious beliefs and understandings which no doubt form a meaningful part of the lives of their many service users (Godina, 2012).

Awura Adjoa was engaged in chores in the home and responded negatively when this was taken away from her. It is reasonable to assume that this may not have been the case with a male child of a similar age, a view supported by Dotti Sani (2016), who concluded that housework is a gendered process. Awura Adjoa's stepmother and step-grandmother played significant roles in her maltreatreatment while her teacher and school nurse, both female, acted in supportive and caring ways. The attitude and behaviour of her stepmother and step-grandmother did not fit with the stereotype and image of women as caring, forgiving, nurturing and loving. On the other hand, the stereotype of *wicked stepmother* was validated in this narrative.

In a study undertaken by Hanisch and Moulding (2011), a social worker suggested that there should be an emphasis on power relations between adults and children because women, like men, can be perpetrators of abuse. Ter Haar (2007, p 62) argued that witchcraft is often used to '*enforce rigid gender roles*'.

Awura Adjoa's father and their pastor (both male) were the ones who ultimately determined her fate: the pastor's revelation that she was a witch, and her father informing her of her return to West Africa. Again, the roles of these two men reinforced the notion of a gender hierarchy where the authority for decision-making resided with Awura Adjoa's father and pastor.

We invite you to consider additional theoretical perspectives and/or concepts linked to Awura Adjoa's narrative.

SOCIAL WORK PROFESSIONAL REQUIREMENTS

In this section, we identify social work professional requirements that align with the content of Awura Adjoa's narrative and the book as a whole. With a protected title, social work continues to be a crucial and relevant profession which is globally recognised and valued. The requirements which will be discussed here include:

- the Professional Capabilities Framework;
- the HCPC standards of proficiency;
- knowledge and skills statement;
- social work values and code of ethics.

Professional Capabilities Framework (PCF)

The PCF was introduced in 2013 and is the overarching framework underpinning professional social work practice (BASW, 2014). It is unique in that it is applicable across all stages and levels of social work practice at pre-qualifying and post-qualifying stages. It is an important consideration for social work students or qualified practitioners who are trying to understand and work with families where children have been labelled or are at risk of being labelled witches. The framework highlights nine domains which have been discussed below and identifies how each domain fits with elements of Awura Adjoa's narrative.

1. **Professionalism**

Being professional in this context relates to acting and behaving in a manner that is consistent with professional values and principles in social work. It involves recognising that the title *social worker* is protected and that conduct and behaviour which is not consistent with the profession will be sanctioned. In working with Awura Adjoa and her family, a social worker would be expected to introduce themselves formally and outline their role and responsibilities.

2. **Rights, Justice and Economic Well-being: Advance human rights, and promote social justice and economic well-being**

A children's rights framework has been proposed as a useful strategy to make sense of and understand the need to challenge this practice (Tedam, 2014). Children have the right to be safe and protected from harm; therefore, it is clear that the treatment meted out to Awura Adjoa is not in keeping with principles of social justice and human rights and was a clear infringement on her rights as a child. For example, the emotional trauma which she appeared to face on a daily basis, coupled with the lack of consultation with her in relation to the various moves, transitions and the return to West Africa, are also not in keeping with principles of justice and fairness.

3. **Knowledge: Apply knowledge of social sciences, law and social work practice theory**

Theories of family systems, labelling, stigma, attachment and human growth and development have all been used to explore ways in which witchcraft-related abuse might be understood. More importantly, an attempt has been made to link the experiences described by Awura Adjoa with concepts and theoretical perspectives which social workers could draw upon while working with cases of this nature. For example, relevant legal and policy frameworks such as the Children Act 1989, Children Act 2004, and the Human Rights Act 1998 have been discussed, as have the broader issues of immigration, race and racism and skills required for effective working with children and families from black and minority ethnic families.

4. **Critical Reflection and Analysis: Apply critical reflection and analysis to inform and provide a rationale for professional decision-making**

It has been suggested by Streets (2009, p 192) that 'conscientious social workers do not arrive at their personal or professional position regarding very complex and ethically and morally challenging issues easily or hastily'. Awura Adjoa's narrative has provided areas for critical thinking and reflection. Social workers need to have an enquiring mind and are expected to be able to provide a critical analysis of the information that is presented to them in relation to a given case. Supervision could be used as a space which enables critical reflection on a multitude of issues which have been highlighted through this narrative. Additionally, Wilkins and Boahen (2013) suggest that critical analysis involves the 'application of reason and logic' (p 47) and also suggest that there is a role for intuition and emotion.

5. **Intervention and Skills: Use judgement and authority to intervene with individuals, families and communities to promote independence, provide support and prevent harm, neglect and abuse**

Social workers have a duty to protect vulnerable people from harm and to actively promote the safety and well-being of children and other vulnerable groups. Awura Adjoa's experiences were never identified or exposed; nonetheless, we can speculate that if her abuse had become known to social workers, they would have intervened to prevent her from being harmed any further and would have considered the well-being of her siblings. The intervention would have had to be undertaken with the whole family and possibly members of the community and faith leaders. Trevithick (2005) has proposed useful interventional skills which would be relevant when working with Awura Adjoa and her family: for example, challenging and confronting; negotiating skills; mediation and advocacy skills.

6.   **Professional Leadership: Take responsibility for the professional learning and development of others through supervision, mentoring, assessing, research, teaching, leadership and management**

In a situation where a social worker may be unfamiliar with this form of child maltreatment, they might find it useful to discuss this with their supervisor and to seek relevant training which will enhance their understanding of how to effectively engage with children and families experiencing this form of abuse. Tsui (2005) recognises the significance of supervision which holds educational and supportive value for social workers. The dyad involved in this supervision are the social worker and their supervisor/manager and both should be prepared to give and take. Workforce development teams in local authorities and in the voluntary and independent sectors need to consult with social work managers about the learning and development needs of their practitioners.

7.   **Values and Ethics: Apply social work ethical principles and values to guide professional practice**

In order to effectively work with Awura Adjoa, a social worker would have to ensure that they are working in accordance with principles and values that are ethical. For example, being non-judgemental would require a social worker to be able to stand back and listen to Awura Adjoa's experiences without pre-judging the outcome based on her race, ethnicity, religious beliefs, age, gender, migration history etc. The code of ethics for social work, BASW (2012), would have to be strictly adhered to, recognising that social workers have to work within organisational boundaries which sometimes create ethical dilemmas in practice. For example, how might a social worker address and support Awura Adjoa's needs in relation to her faith when it became apparent that her pastor was condoning and possibly encouraging some of the treatment that Awura Adjoa was receiving from her parents? Might this be particularly uncomfortable for a social worker of a similar faith?

8.   **Diversity: Recognise diversity and apply anti-discriminatory and anti-oppressive principles in practice**

Recognising and respecting diversity is the first step towards appreciating the relevance of anti-discriminatory and anti-oppressive practice in social work. Social workers are advised to probe individuals and families '*about religious matters*' even when families do not '*spontaneously raise these issues*' (Pargament, 1997, p 374). Social workers are required to explain to their service users the rationale and purpose of their intervention and should be able to provide answers to any questions that families may have about social services involvement and the assessment process.

A social worker involved with Awura Adjoa and her family would be expected to maintain a fair position, working with the facts and evidence in the case. There are many aspects of Awura Adjoa's identity which might result in her being discriminated against – these include her age, gender, ethnicity, race, migration history, and so on. Working with a social worker from a BME background may not result in a more effective outcome for

Awura Adjoa as there are many more areas of difference which could impact on the working relationship. Bernard and Harris (2016, p 17) caution social workers about not falling into the trap of explaining black children's experiences in terms of *'cultural relativism'*, which historically has resulted in these children being under-protected.

9. **Professional Leadership**

Social workers at every stage of their studies and practice when qualified must demonstrate leadership skills. Using the narrative of Awura Adjoa, a social worker would have to ensure that they know what is required and can be self-directive in their approach to working with Awura Adjoa and her family. For example, leadership is demonstrated when a social worker can manage the case of Awura Adjoa right from the initial stages and through the process of assessment and engagement. In addition, a social worker can demonstrate leadership qualities by being innovative and critical in their approach.

HCPC standards of proficiency

The standards of proficiency (SoPs; HCPC online, 2017) articulate quite clearly what social workers need to know and be able to do at the point of qualification.

While these SoPs are constantly under review and revision, their currency requires us to take note of how they might have been used to enhance social work practice with Awura Adjoa. The SoPs discussed below are the most current (HCPC online, 2017).

Be able to draw on appropriate knowledge and skills to inform practice	Understanding witchcraft labelling, the impact of emotional and physical abuse, understanding BME and faith communities, anti-discriminatory practice (ADP)/anti-racist practise (ARP) and anti-oppressive practice (AOP).
Understand the key concepts of the knowledge base relevant to their profession	ADP/ARP/AOP. Theories, methods and models.
Be able to reflect on and review practice	Using supervision and peer mentoring. Acknowledging gaps in knowledge. Research.
Be able to practise in a non-discriminatory manner	Use your knowledge and role to discuss and disrupt any existing discriminatory or oppressive practices by professionals working with the family. Also acknowledge the internal workings of discriminatory parenting practices according to age, gender etc.

Be able to communicate effectively	Use age-appropriate language with Awura Adjoa, taking into consideration the fact that she has recently arrived from West Africa. Use a language-specific interpreter, preferably one who has experience of interpreting in relation to this form of abuse.
Be aware of the impact of culture, equality and diversity on practice	Understanding various family systems and dynamics. Cultural sensitivity and competence.
Be able to practise within the legal and ethical boundaries of their profession	Children Act 1989 and 2004, Human Rights Act 1998 are useful legislation which could be used in work with Awura Adjoa and her family Also consider the ethical principles of social work.
Understand the need to establish and maintain a safe practice environment	Ensure practitioner safety. Recognise the safety needs of Awura Adjoa in the home environment, in her place of worship and in school.
Be able to maintain records appropriately	Ensure notes taken of meetings with Awura Adjoa and her family are accurate and stored confidentially. These will need to be updated regularly and shared with relevant professionals as per interagency guidelines.
Be able to assure the quality of their practice	Practitioners need to ensure they use supervision appropriately and review the quality of their work through periodic audits and evaluations. Feedback from Awura Adjoa, her family and other professionals can enhance the quality of practice.
Be able to work appropriately with others	Build and maintain good working relationships with Awura Adjoa, her family, faith leader/elder, community members (if appropriate) and other professionals from the statutory and voluntary sectors (Education, Health, AFRUCA, VCF)

Another area for consideration is the global definition of social work and how it relates to the narrative contained within this book.

Social work is a practice-based profession and an academic discipline that promotes social change and development, social cohesion, and the empowerment and liberation of people. Principles of social justice, human rights, collective responsibility and respect for diversities are central to social work. Underpinned by theories of social work, social sciences, humanities and indigenous knowledge, social work engages people and structures to address life challenges and enhance wellbeing.

(IFSW, 2014)

> ## REFLECTIVE QUESTION
>
> In what ways do you consider that Awura Adjoa's narrative can be understood within the context of the global definition of social work above?

The term *environment* in social work refers to social systems to which people belong and these influence their situations, conditions and outcomes. Social workers would need to pay particular attention to the people within Awura Adjoa's environment. In her particular case, this involves many uncles, aunties, grandparents, pastors and friends of the family.

Research suggests that over the last few years, children and young people have articulated their understanding of their well-being to be more subjective than objective (Statham and Chase, 2010). In this regard, Awura Adjoa reflects on three main ingredients which she feels creates a happy childhood for children and enhances their well-being. These, she says are '*love*', '*a happy home*' and being '*burden free*' and she concludes that the absence of these in her childhood led to what she has described as an unhappy childhood.

A range of social work skills, principles and intervention techniques are required to work with a child such as Awura Adjoa and her family to facilitate change and enhance social and community cohesion. It is entirely possible that the involvement of a church or faith group referred to in Awura Adjoa's narrative could have led to tensions among members of this church and/or community group and could possibly have resulted in the further isolation and exclusion of Awura Adjoa and her family. It is therefore imperative that any interventions planned for this family should be culturally sensitive (Akilapa and Simkiss, 2012), respectful, transparent and honest to avoid the family and/or Awura Adjoa going underground. Martin (2011) suggests that social workers need to have excellent communication skills which involve active listening and interacting, while Moss et al (2005) caution against the use of power which can undermine and alter communication.

Knowledge and skills statement

The knowledge and skills statement (KSS) proposed by the review into social work education (DfE, 2014) and currently recognised by HEIs and social work employers requires social workers in the children and families specialism to be able to effectively demonstrate the ten key areas listed below. They are:

- relationships and effective direct work;
- communication;
- child development;
- adult mental ill health, substance misuse, domestic abuse, physical ill health and disability;

- abuse and neglect of children;
- child and family assessment;
- analysis, decision-making, planning and review;
- the law and the family and youth justice systems;
- the role of supervision;
- organisational context.

Awura Adjoa's narrative therefore should be considered within the context of the KSS and by both pre- and post-qualified social workers.

REFLECTIVE QUESTION

How might a social worker relate the elements of the KSS to Awura Adjoa's narrative?

Social work values and code of ethics

It has been argued that poor preparation on social work programmes and minimal support from supervisors and managers could mean that practitioners feel less confident in exploring religious or spirituality practices with families (Horwath and Lees, 2010). A reminder of the values which social workers sign up to is required to understand them within the context of this very specific safeguarding concern (BASW online).

While the entirety of these will not be rehearsed within this book, there are a few which will be: human rights, social justice, professional integrity and principles of fairness and non-oppression.

PRACTICE DILEMMA

How would you approach working with Awura Adjoa if as a practitioner you believe in witchcraft and spirit possession?

We considered that it might be useful to address this practice dilemma in a proactive way rather than provide a set of questions and/or issues for readers to consider and discuss on their own. We recognise that the growing diversity of the social work workforce could mean that there will be practitioners who either believe that children can be witches or may have other beliefs that could impact on their work with service users where this is the case. Akhtar (2013) cautions that for practitioners who experience a dissonance between their personal beliefs and professional duties and responsibilities, a values matrix could be a useful tool to assist in unpicking some of these conflicts. The values matrix provides an uncomplicated way of examining a practice dilemma such as this.

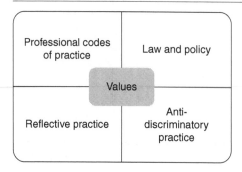

Figure 8.3   Values matrix (Akhtar, 2013, p 16)

In addition to the values matrix (Akhtar, 2013), there are a number of strategies which social workers and other childcare professionals may wish to introduce or continue in their daily practice. These are:

- the use of supervision;
- critical reflection;
- reflexivity;
- emotional intelligence.

Beddoe et al (2014, p 119) propose that supervision is '*a safe place to employ and strengthen the personal attributes of supervisees*', which therefore positively impacts on the practitioner's well-being.

In addition, social workers who may hold similar beliefs must use reflection critically if they are to address and disrupt a way of thinking that may have negative consequences for the very children and vulnerable people they are trying to protect. In this regard, Schon's concepts of *reflection in action* and *on action* may be a useful starting point for any social worker. *Reflection in action* requires social workers to think on their feet and as they are interacting and intervening in the lives of service users. Schon's second form of reflection is *reflection on action*, where a social worker will consider action which has recently occurred and try to understand how they might have approached things differently and how they might intervene on another occasion.

Thompson and Pascal (2012) propose a third form of reflection, *reflection for action*, which refers to thinking ahead or forethought. It refers to the '*process of planning, thinking ahead about what is to come, so that we can draw on our experience in order to make the best use of the time resources available*' (p 317).

The weather model of reflection (Maclean, 2016) could be used by practitioners to understand what went well, what did not go well, surprises and barriers to their intervention in a case of witchcraft labelling. In particular, the barriers to intervention would be an important area to focus on during supervision as this may illuminate where a social worker's values and beliefs impact on their practice.

Finch et al (2013) propose the term *diminished reflection* to refer to a decrease in reflective capacity when professionals '*are overwhelmed with a range of intensively distressing and disturbing emotions that they cannot digest*'. For a social worker who may hold similar beliefs, when confronted with Awura Adjoa and her family, they could feel a sense of '*guilt, fear, hopelessness and dread*' (p 8).

Reflexivity was described by Fook (1999) as the ability to recognise our influence as well as the influence of our social and cultural contexts on research and practice. Social workers should understand the way in which their own position on issues of witchcraft may impact on their practice and should acknowledge this on an ongoing basis through supervision and personal development plans.

Stone (2016) describes emotional intelligence as the ability to understand '*our emotional responses to situations and being able to keep them in check*'. This, she argues will enable social workers to respond professionally and appropriately to situations with their service users while avoiding the '*emotional labour*' (p 52) which can be present in a practitioner who is not emotionally intelligent.

It is crucial that social workers who believe in witchcraft act within the law and their professional ethics and values. They must have regard for their professional registration and be aware of the ongoing registration requirements by the HCPC and/or other regulatory bodies.

FURTHER READING

Akhtar, F (2013) Mastering Social Work Values and Ethics. *London. Jessica Kingsley Publishers.*

Stone, C (2016) Fostering Emotional Intelligence Within Social Work Practice, in Stone, C and Harbin, F (eds) Transformative Learning for Social Work: Learning For and In Practice. *London. Palgrave.*

CHAPTER SUMMARY

This chapter has presented theoretical reflections based on Awura Adjoa's narrative. It has outlined some key theories and professional requirements for social workers. It has also made reference to other professions where appropriate.

Frameworks for recognition and response

This chapter will examine some of the existing practice frameworks which social workers and other childcare practitioners could use to recognise and respond to this form of abuse. As social workers go through rigorous academic and practice assessment, it would be unwise to omit frameworks for assisting in the teaching of this area of growing concern in professional qualifying programmes. Consequently, three frameworks will be examined:

- framework for teaching and learning about witchcraft labelling;
- framework for assessing labelled children and their families;
- framework for engaging with children and their families.

FRAMEWORK FOR TEACHING AND LEARNING ABOUT WITCHCRAFT LABELLING

Recruitment efforts in recent years have resulted in an increase in the number of black minority ethnic (BME) students attending universities in the UK. The rise is significant, from 14.9 per cent in 2004 to 17.2 per cent in 2009 (Weekes-Barnard, 2010). It has also been suggested that social work enrolments by BME students in 2012/13 stood at 27 per cent (3,180) for undergraduate programmes and 26 per cent (375 students) for enrolment on graduate social work programmes in English HEIs (HEFCE online data).

More recently, these figures have increased significantly with 30.3 per cent of black and Asian minority ethnic students enrolled onto social work courses in 2015 (Skills for Care, 2016).

As social work education in England continues to experience change, it is important that educators in the sector remain focused on the protection and safeguarding of vulnerable people by ensuring teaching and learning strategies are evidenced, informed and can respond to the changes in demographics.

It has been argued that if social workers encourage only dominant groups to engage in knowledge creation, then social work students will be taught the knowledge and skills used by dominant groups (Figueira-McDonough et al, 2001).

This section will focus on some ideas about how social work educators (in the classroom and in practice) can ensure issues that may affect ethnic minority service users are not neglected in the delivery of social work education. The work of Bourdieu in relation to *habitus* is an important consideration for social work academics and educators. Bourdieu (1991) viewed educational institutions as settings where people play to different power dynamics, mostly within the context of the middle classes and the elite. Students who are in similar cultural categories to their educators could possess an advantage over 'other' students. The disadvantage then is when these categories and cultural capital are reproduced. In order to meet the needs of the growing diversity of service users, educators need to ensure that they activate the cultural capital in their students (Merolla and Jackson, 2014) to view learning about other ethnicities and cultures as added value to their knowledge base and not as burdensome or unnecessary.

A module or unit which focuses on *working with difference*, *diversity* or *anti-oppressive and anti-discriminatory practice* would appear to be an appropriate place for subjects such as witchcraft abuse to be located and taught. However, it is important that educators support students to understand the interconnections with and relevance for other modules such as sociology, psychology, social policy and law and its application to practice learning, for example. These modules should have clear learning outcomes which would assist students in understanding the rationale for the inclusion of some discrete areas of knowledge such as witchcraft labelling.

For post-qualifying social work or CPD, specific workshops and seminars around this topic could be held with organisations such as AFRUCA, VCF and BASW at the forefront of such specialist training and knowledge dissemination.

Undoubtedly, there is direct relevance for a multi-disciplinary approach to developing the practitioner knowledge base on the issues identified and addressed within this book. Professionals who might benefit from this training include education staff (including teachers, teaching assistants, early childhood other support staff, breakfast and after-school club workers).

In the area of health, training could be adapted for school nurses, GPs, mental health professionals, children's nurses, and specialist doctors. There is evidence to suggest that one advantage of learning together is that closer relationships can be forged between and among professionals who are trying to safeguard children. Additionally, a clearer understanding of the different professional roles and responsibilities could be gained through interprofessional learning and education (O'Carroll et al, 2016).

It has been suggested by Anghel and Ramon (2009) that the UK is the only country where social work education is mandated to include service user involvement; however, there have been concerns that there are '*marginalised service user groups*' (Irvine et al, 2015, p 140) who are conspicuous by their absence in the social work curriculum.

In my professional experience to date as a social worker and as an academic, Awura Adjoa is the first person to share her experiences of witchcraft labelling in the manner she has and as such it would be fair to conclude that her experiences would not be 'typical' of the service users invited to contribute to social work education at UK HEIs. Awura Adjoa's experience would be insightful and useful to students at all levels and stages of social work education, especially given the fact that the students in Irvine et al's (2015) study reported that they would have liked to have met service users from a wide range of cultures and experiences as they did not feel that the ones they had contact with through their universities were representative of the '*real world*' (p 144).

In the situation where Awura Adjoa is unable to be physically present to share her experiences, the relevant areas of her narrative could be used to develop case studies, vignettes and other learning resources which could be used in the teaching of social work students and/or post-qualifying CPD candidates.

Having identified health and education professionals as potential readers of this book, it is appropriate to highlight the significance of multi-agency and collaborative practice and to consider ways in which a range of professionals might benefit from shared learning and practice in this area.

Everyone working or in contact with children has a responsibility to recognise and know how to act on evidence, concerns, and signs that a child's health, development and safety is or may be being impaired, especially when they suffer or are at risk of significant harm.

(DCSF, 2010, p 2)

There is also the need to recognise where and how this knowledge might be useful in practice teaching and learning. Social work practice educators could use Awura Adjoa's narrative to provide students with opportunities for critical reflection, discussion and analysis. There is a list of voluntary sector organisations which have provided placements for social work students in the past and may be willing to do so in the future (Appendix 2). Placements in these organisations will further students with a range of learning opportunities in areas not routinely taught on social work qualifying programmes.

FRAMEWORK FOR ASSESSING LABELLED CHILDREN AND THEIR FAMILIES

Crisp et al (2003) have argued in favour of the importance of graduating social workers being able to understand the principles of assessment and have highlighted useful principles to assist in achieving this. In this section, the main question we are seeking to answer is: '*How might a qualified social worker or social work student on placement assess Awura Adjoa in the context of her narrative?*'

It is useful to begin with a discussion about assessments more broadly. Assessment is an ongoing process, fluid and dynamic and cannot be a single event (Martin, 2011) and if we are to use the lived experience of Awura Adjoa as the basis of an assessment, it somewhat validates this perspective. There is no point at which the assessment could have been discontinued or have been concluded. From the time she arrived in the UK and for the two years she lived in the UK, a social worker would have been able to undertake an assessment as an ongoing process, identifying and adding to the many areas of concern.

Briggs et al (2011) have suggested that existing categories of abuse (neglect, emotional, sexual and physical abuse) are a useful framework for understanding witchcraft abuse. *The Framework for the Assessment of Children in Need and Their Families* (DoH, 2000) can also be used to gain further understanding of the family circumstances because, as Furness and Gilligan (2010) suggest, there is little need for additional assessment frameworks aimed at assessing families where faith and religion may be areas of concern as this is neither time and cost effective nor beneficial to service users.

The framework for assessment proposed by Furness and Gilligan (2010) consists of eight questions which should prompt discussion and reflection about a service user's religious affiliations and how they practise their beliefs. Details of this framework can be found in their book; however, by way of summary, they encourage practitioners to develop an open, trusting and respectful relationship with their service users, to consider their own religiosity (or otherwise) and to approach each family with an openness and preparedness to review assumptions. In addition, the framework proposes that social workers should actively seek to update their own knowledge of spiritual or religious beliefs which may be unfamiliar to them. In general terms, the framework promotes a person-centred approach and should be considered during all stages of the assessment process. This supports the view by Bernard and Gupta (2008) who advocate the use of empowering language and positive non-judgemental attitudes when working with ethnic minority families. They argue that any intervention with BME families which begins from a deficit or pathological lens can contribute to oppressive practice. Godina (2012) has warned against the tick-box exercises in the area of religion and faith and discourages social workers from avoiding discussion in this area.

Barn and Kirton (2016) have cautioned against bracketing off the abuse linked to spirit possession and witchcraft labelling from mainstream discussions about physical and other forms of abuse. For that reason, we propose our own framework, Witchcraft Labelling Assessment Framework (WLAF), as an additional resource to assist with the identification, assessment and provision of support to families where children may be at risk of witchcraft labelling. WLAF draws directly from the experiences of Awura Adjoa and in conjunction with some of the theoretical and practice frameworks which exist in contemporary social work practice.

For practitioners who are using the Framework for the Assessment of Children in Need and their Families, Common Assessment Framework (CAF), Early Help Assessment (EHA) or specific national or local assessment tools and frameworks, WLAF could be used during the discussion and exploration of the various elements of these frameworks to draw out further information from families. WLAF should not be seen as an end in itself and should be used in conjunction with the other frameworks already mentioned (see Appendix 1). Identifying children who may be at risk of significant harm and subsequently protecting them involves working with families to create safer and enabling places for children (Munro and Hubbard, 2011).

FRAMEWORK FOR ENGAGING WITH LABELLED CHILDREN AND FAMILIES

Social workers are required to embrace diversity and work with people from a range of socio-economic, cultural and linguistic backgrounds. The profession prides itself in its aims of advocating on behalf of service users, empowering vulnerable people and supporting them to work through life's challenges and difficulties, which include harm, transitions, loss and grief, disability and so on. Social workers can only achieve this by working effectively with service users and their families.

When assessments have concluded that a child is at risk of witchcraft labelling, social workers need to understand how they might engage or work with the child and their family.

Culturally competent practice is '*one of the greatest challenges in the social work profession*' Laird (2008, p 159) asserts, and this is because it is difficult to define. The definition by Walker (2005, p 31) is one that is widely used in the UK context. It defines cultural competence as '*a set of knowledge-based and interpersonal skills that allows individuals to understand, appreciate and work with families of cultures other than their own*'. It has been suggested elsewhere (Tedam, 2013) that the use of a framework such as the cultural web could enable social workers to focus on the unique elements within a family and tease out information which would be useful in any assessment. The cultural web is also compatible with the PCF. Adapted from the culturagram by Parker and Bradley (2010), the cultural web is unique in that it also acknowledges the complex nature of family forms and relationships. It could be argued that, in the case of Awura Adjoa, immediate and extended family 'relatives' were never in short supply, exacerbated by her father introducing them as *aunt, uncle, grandmother* and *grandfather*, and came in a range of ages and genders.

It has to be stated though that culture is not static, it is fluid, and should not be divorced from a child's other needs (Allain, 2007).

Ethnic minority families living in the UK, according to Ochieng (2003), have historically used the term '*extended family*' to describe their kinship and living arrangements, yet she argues that this concept is poorly understood. She suggests that extended families exist in these communities to provide financial, emotional and physical support in many aspects of life. She views childcare and child-minding as part of the areas of support provided.

Horwath and Lees (2010) posit that there is sufficient evidence highlighting religious beliefs as presenting social workers with challenges in their daily practice; consequently, it is important that they '*develop a genuine curiosity about religion and its impact on people's lives*' (Godina, 2012, p 388).

This must extend beyond the well-established ticking of boxes indicating whether a parent, child or young person is of a particular religion. There needs to be a systematic examination of parental values and goals of parenting that acknowledges the cultural and religious diversity of UK citizens alongside an exploration of the impact that a distinctive religious context has on children and young people growing up (Padilla-Walker and Thompson, 2005).

Mays (2000) states that, '*No one should have their future, their health, or their well-being compromised for reasons of class, gender, national origin, physical and psychological abilities, religion, or sexual orientation, or as a result of unfair distribution of resources*' (p 326). Any intervention with Awura Adjoa therefore must seek to empower through being supportive, understanding and empathetic. Practice which has the potential to *retraumatise* should be avoided (Hooper and Warwick, 2006).

It must also be highlighted that while the assessment and intervention is ongoing with the family, supervision becomes a key determinant of how effectively the practitioner will engage while continuously reflecting upon and developing their practice.

The importance of supervision for practitioners who work with these types of concerns therefore cannot be overemphasised. Good quality supervision undertaken regularly provides the space and opportunity for discussions and support for the social work practitioner.

There have been some attempts to understand religion and spirituality in the context of social care practice with children and their families. For example, Mathews (2009) argues that social work is disadvantaged by its infrequent mention of and engagement with religion and spirituality. He reinforces the benefits of understanding religion and spirituality in order to better assess what motivates our service users on a daily basis. Clearly not all people who come into contact with social work services are religious; however, Mathews (2009) is of the view that many more people are spiritual because spirituality is usually expressed in the way people view the world.

After engaging with the contents of this book, the critical question should be:

What should social workers do when a child, their family or friends believe they possess witchcraft?

As has already been discussed, the area of witchcraft labelling is complex, sensitive and dynamic in terms of its effects, impact and manifestation globally and in the UK. It is entirely possible that depending on where a social worker is practising, they may never come across a case of witchcraft labelling in their career. Nonetheless, given the ever-growing diversity of ethnicities, faiths and beliefs in the UK, it may be that a social worker becomes involved in a case where a family's belief systems result in safeguarding concerns for children and other vulnerable adults – for example, an adult with disabilities whose family believe that their disability is a result of witchcraft and who appear not to be engaging with medical/health care professionals. Such a situation would give rise to assessment and intervention arising from the implications of the belief, not the belief itself.

Social workers must be prepared to work 'with' the belief and not against it. The issue they seek most to address is the behaviours which might result from the belief system and which may be abusive or harmful to a child or vulnerable adult.

It may also be in the profession's best interest to attempt to understand that individual, family and community beliefs can influence behaviours and attitudes and so it may be important to seek to understand family and community beliefs and ideologies before any meaningful interventions can occur.

It may be important to understand the differences between collectivist and individualist communities because research undertaken by Triandis (1995) suggested that people from ethnic minority backgrounds tend to generalise reasons for their behaviour using culture, faith/religion or community. On the other hand, white British participants often attributed their behaviour to their upbringing or personality. Such an understanding is crucial if social workers are to build trust and develop positive working relationships with children and their families.

Social workers should draw upon the relevant legislative, policy, assessment and intervention frameworks to guide their practice. Supervision, peer support and enhancing their knowledge and skills through training is strongly advised. Ultimately, social workers should engage in practice which is relationship-based, person-centred and anti-oppressive.

Recognising that the child is part of a wider system gives legitimacy to the use of a cosmological model (Doyle and Timms, 2014) which seeks to understand the physical, cognitive, emotional, social, spiritual and moral development of a child over time.

10 Lessons learnt and conclusion

Serious case reviews (SCRs) and child death inquiries have a lot to teach us; however, The Department for Education (2016c) has suggested that not all learning from SCRs is implemented. There have been many instances where childcare professionals have either missed opportunities to intervene or where they have intervened, they may have incorrectly assessed the children and families.

In this narrative, we have identified opportunities where statutory and voluntary sector organisations could have become involved to disrupt the abuse which was occurring. The narrative has also evidenced that the labelling of children as witches is not new and that about 20 years ago at least one child in the UK suffered such unacceptable pain and trauma.

This final chapter will bring together four dominant themes which have emerged from Awura Adjoa's narrative and appear to be pivotal to contemporary social work policy and practice. These themes are: parents, parenting, family and friends; the role of faith organisations and church leaders; school teachers and the local education authority, travel and transitions.

The chapter will conclude with our definition of witchcraft labelling.

PARENTS, PARENTING, FAMILY AND FRIENDS

Jones (2010) has outlined the need for *good enough* parenting by suggesting that it refers to being able to meet a child's psychological, educational and emotional needs, as well as ensuring quality physical care and the provision of adequate supervision and protection from harm. Awura Adjoa's parents did not appear to be able to provide her with consistent love, care and affection to meet her needs. It is also acknowledged that there appeared to be little preparation leading up to her reuniting with her family and that this resulted in her stepmother questioning the upbringing Awura Adjoa had received in West Africa.

Family and friends who became a part of this narrative may not have recognised the need for intervention at the time. It could be that they may not have wanted to appear to be 'taking sides' while the accusations and labelling were going on. It is important, for safe-guarding purposes, that family and friends take more of an active role in ensuring children are safe rather than taking the position of unconcerned bystanders and observers.

It may also be the case that at the very least, they could have considered an anonymous referral to children's social care who could have provided guidance at that point. Of particular concern are the extended family members who appeared to be around Awura Adjoa and who she referred to as *step-grandmother, auntie* and *uncle.*

Awura Adjoa confirms that her older siblings were at university and so a social worker would need to consider what (if anything) they knew about Awura Adjoa's circumstances and experiences and whether this places her other siblings at risk of significant harm.

Closely linked to this discussion is the possibility of a private fostering arrangement when Awura Adjoa was sent to live with her step-grandmother. As far back as the late 1960s, there were reported to be around 6000 children of West African origin in private fostering arrangements (Ellis, 1977), of whom very little was known. It was not until the untimely death of Victoria Climbié in 2000 that private fostering came into focus again, this time resulting in legislation to ensure that children who were in such arrangements were known to the authorities. There was also the requirement to undertake an assessment of their contributions to a child's well-being and development. Currently, there is a duty to notify the local authority when a child is living with a non-blood relation for more than 28 days.

THE ROLE OF FAITH ORGANISATIONS AND CHURCH LEADERS

Central to any discussion of witchcraft labelling linked to faith is the consideration of the role of faith organisations and church leaders.

Research suggests that in situations where children have been labelled witches, it can be difficult for other people to intervene, particularly where a child has been officially and formally labelled a witch by a pastor or church leader. Pastors and faith leaders hold significant positions of respect within most ethnic minority communities and members of their congregation value and believe what their pastors and church leaders propagate. Awura Adjoa's parents appeared to believe in the power of the faith leader and consequently allowed themselves to be convinced that their daughter was a witch and that some form of further church attendance and intervention might clear Awura Adjoa of the alleged witchcraft.

The evidence suggests that religion has a significant place in the lives of African families; consequently, it is important to remember the need for interagency and collaborative working, particularly with church communities and other faith-based groups. It is also important to recognise that not all church and faith activities take place within the context of a fixed space or building called a church. Instead, it is becoming increasingly popular to hold faith services and prayer group meetings in the private homes of some of the church members and leaders. This sort of prayer and service leaves vulnerable children at risk of further exploitation due to the fact that the home is regarded as a private sphere and there is perhaps less scrutiny of people coming in and going out of any home.

There are growing groups of people who choose to meet and hold religious services in people's private homes at various points and times during the week. This sort of process is open to abuse because there is very little that can be done about regulation and scrutiny. The Churches' Child Protection Advisory Service (CCPAS) and other organisations require churches to be duly registered and signed up to child protection and safeguarding processes and procedures. There is also a duty on faith groups and churches to ensure that people who work with children and young people are adequately trained and security cleared to undertake the work expected of them. These provisions are undermined when church services are held in the homes and front rooms of its members. In order to properly ensure the well-being of children in formal church buildings and in other forms of religious arrangements, it is important to realign the regulations with the requirements of child safeguarding.

This is what Woods (2013, p 1062) refers to as a '*house-church*', which he suggests is common in Sri Lanka and which provides evangelical groups with autonomy and a degree of self-empowerment. These arrangements have arisen largely in response to environments which are hostile to religion and which challenge religious freedom. Consequently, house-churches are by design clandestine and secret arrangements which are not meant to be visible or obvious and so do not have visible signs of the faith. The fact that this sort of arrangement is organised does not mean it is immune to many of the issues which churches can be faced with. Indeed, these arrangements appear to be fertile grounds in which some of the worst forms of abuse could occur.

It is also worth noting that Awura Adjoa's parents first took her to see their pastor outside standard church times. Awura Adjoa recalls '*going down some stairs which took us to the inside of what felt like a hole and where the church took place. Going down the stairs felt like going underground.*' This was not the family's regular place of worship and we do not wish to speculate on the reasons for Awura Adjoa's parents' choice of this particular church and pastor.

Critical to this discussion is the added dimension of the subsequent practice of taking Awura Adjoa to church during the week and in addition to the usual Sunday service. It is important to note that none of her siblings were required to attend weekday church services.

SCHOOL TEACHERS/EDUCATION AUTHORITIES

Awura Adjoa's outward appearance, despite her trying her hardest, occasionally revealed that of an unhappy child. The argument has already been made that the school authorities were quick to conclude that Awura Adjoa's behaviour was as a result of bullies, instead of perhaps asking her what exactly was going on and/or informing her parents about it. For example, Awura Adjoa falling asleep in lessons should have been more robustly examined. It is acknowledged that currently schools work to comprehensive guidance about dealing with bullying and so in today's practice, the issue of bullying would have been more stringently addressed. It is also important that any change of residential address and/or change of name of main carer, for example, is investigated to ensure continued safeguarding of all children and vulnerable children in particular. It does not appear that the school authorities were aware of the change of Awura Adjoa's residence to that of her step-grandmother. Again, with current practice, it may be possible for the school to find out about Awura Adjoa's change of address, although it appears that schools do not routinely ask for this information unless they are concerned about a child or children. Schools tend to rely on parents and carers to self-report any changes in their circumstances and living arrangements.

Awura Adjoa's narrative suggests that the only people who saw her regularly, outside her family, were at school and church. This makes it all the more critical that in current practice, the school nurse and/or teachers would need to be making further enquiries about her home environment, which may have led them to uncover her change of address.

In addition to the above, the duration of her stay with her step-grandmother could have resulted in a private fostering assessment to ensure that Awura Adjoa would be safe and secure. Her parents and wider family did not appear to have considered the impact of the change in living arrangements on Awura Adjoa.

Obadina (2012) argues that the role of the school nurse is largely missing in literature about witchcraft labelling; however, Awura Adjoa's narrative clearly identifies opportunities for the school nurse to have become involved. In fact, the school nurse appeared to get close to the presenting issues; however, Awura Adjoa was quick to evade the support offered and declined inviting her parents to the school. We wish to make it clear that Awura Adjoa is unsure about whether the 'school nurse' was a qualified professional or whether this was a shorthand term for the sick bay supervisor or nominated staff member responsible for first aid. Regardless of the exact title of the person who was in this role, safeguarding Awura Adjoa should be prioritised.

Children have repeatedly stated that they expect the adults around them to be vigilant and to notice when things appear to be disturbing or distracting them (Statham and Chase, 2010). They do not necessarily want the burden of having to initiate discussions with the adults around them about how they might be feeling or what might be happening to them. It could be suggested that this was how Awura Adjoa was feeling.

After Awura Adjoa is returned to West Africa, the local education authority in conjunction with her school in the UK appear to have made enquiries about her whereabouts, which is a step in the right direction if we are to safeguard all children, particularly those of school-going age. Worryingly, the school (and local education authority) appeared to be satisfied with seeing photos of Awura Adjoa, which by her own admission were taken when she was well dressed and smiling. It is acknowledged that there may have been little else the school could have done and on that basis, asking for evidence that Awura Adjoa was safe should be commended. Under current practice, the local education authority may have been able to seek support from International Social Services (ISS) in the area of international family mediation to protect Awura Adjoa (ISS online, 2017). In addition, the local authority is able to make enquiries where it is felt the child is at risk of significant harm abroad. Many of these processes are subject to nationality requirements, for example; however, at this time Awura Adjoa was not a British citizen but had Indefinite Leave to Remain in the UK.

It has been suggested by Broadhurst et al (2005) that children who are missing from school are a hard to reach group; consequently, their narratives and the views of their parents and carers are largely absent from academic discourse. They argue that this group of children should be viewed as much more significantly disadvantaged and vulnerable, citing the case of Victoria Climbié who was not known by the LEA.

In 2006, Ofsted undertook targeted inspections of schools and expressed concerns regarding the large numbers of children who were not enrolled in school and whose whereabouts were unknown to officials. Such children are at risk of underachieving, harm, exploitation and radicalisation, and their lack of enrolment in school undermines the safeguarding duty owed to children by schools and education authorities.

TRAVEL AND TRANSITION

Current safeguarding practice demonstrated by immigration officials through the Borders, Citizenship and Immigration Act 2009 places a statutory safeguarding duty on the immigration service to recognise and facilitate the safety of children they come into contact with (Brammer, 2015). It is therefore highly likely that in contemporary times, Awura Adjoa and her chaperones would have been more strictly interrogated at the point of entry into the UK to minimise any concerns around trafficking, illegal immigration and so on. On Awura Adjoa's return to West Africa, again with a 'chaperone', this might have caught the attention of immigration officials. Further discussions with Awura Adjoa may have concluded in her parents being contacted and/or spoken to about her travel, particularly as she was returning against her will and without consultation. The travel arrangements for Awura Adjoa two years earlier and again during her return could have been better handled and organised as she also experienced transitions which she appeared to be unprepared for.

Social workers and other childcare practitioners are being asked to critically examine living arrangements which have been made or which appear to have been made by the parents or carers and which involve young children. In the case of Awura Adjoa, the rationale for moving her to live with her grandmother was that she was a witch and had evil spirits, which meant that her presence within the family home was detrimental to the health and well-being of others in the home. The death of Victoria Climbié and the subsequent enquiry into her death by Lord Laming spelt out the potential difficulties and risks when private living arrangements are made for children. Awura Adjoa's narrative highlights the following transitions and changes she experienced:

- living with five different relatives in West Africa;
- living with Mrs K and family in West Africa and also on arrival in the UK;
- living with her father and stepmother;
- living with her step-grandmother;
- returning to West Africa, living with an uncle on arrival;
- moved to her aunt's home for the longer term.

REFLECTIVE QUESTION

We would like you to consider what you believe to be the impact of multiple moves on the lives of children.

Awura Adjoa's story will no doubt have left its readers with their own thoughts and views about what the outcome might have been if Awura Adjoa had continued to live under such circumstances in the UK. This story, unlike so many others, concludes well, or at least did not have fatal consequences as in the case of some of the children who experienced this form of abuse in the UK (Victoria Climbié, Kristy Bamu, Samira Ullah, Khyra Ishaq, Child B, to name a few).

Within the space of less than three years, Awura Adjoa had a number of major moves (international and local), resulting in a change of primary caregiver at each move. Research suggests that multiple transitions for children can be disadvantageous and distressing (Harper, 2016). In the case of Awura Adjoa, there was little by way of consultation and no involvement in decision-making prior to these moves. She was expected to go along with the decisions that had been made by adults, which appeared to not always be in her best interest.

While this narrative is based on Awura Adjoa's experiences specifically in England, it must be made clear that these issues could occur anywhere within the UK; for this reason it is important for social workers to be abreast of the legislative and policy frameworks specific to their countries.

It is also worth noting that Awura Adjoa did not appear to have access to an adult she could confide in, which should be an area of concern for any social worker who may become involved in similar situations and circumstances. In undertaking direct work with children and young people, it is important that practitioners ask who the child might be able to speak to about their fears and concerns. Where a child is unable to identify anyone within their family and social lives, it could be cause for concern and alarm, especially where discussion and further probing does not yield additional information. It becomes critical then that further discussion and work is undertaken in this area.

The idea for this book came about a year ago when I was approached by Awura Adjoa with her story. She had not previously considered sharing her narrative with anyone; however, she was beginning to feel that some healing and closure would result from reflecting on and sharing her story. Awura Adjoa was also committed to ensuring that other children would be protected from witchcraft labelling and its associated trauma. Her intention is to challenge the notion that witchcraft labelling is new and during the writing of the book suggested that the people around her knew what was going on but that they somehow failed to act to save her.

That Awura Adjoa is today a university graduate demonstrates her extent of resilience; however, this does not excuse the suffering and abuse she encountered growing up nor is it a confirmed template for other children. History has taught us that there will be children who are less able to ensure what happens to them and there is an unknown group who may have conceded to ill-treatment and lost their lives or become permanently damaged as a result of their experiences.

The book concludes that witchcraft labelling is as harmful or perhaps even more harmful and damaging than any other form of abuse because it very easily straddles all four defined categories of abuse.

Figure 10.1   Witchcraft labelling: sources and impact

We invite you to add to the wordle in Figure 10.1 from your reading of Awura Adjoa's narrative.

DEFINING WITCHCRAFT LABELLING

This book has sought to examine witchcraft labelling and the impact on children, drawing upon the experiences of Awura Adjoa. The authors wish to offer their definition of witchcraft labelling:

Witchcraft labelling is a process by which children or other vulnerable people experience physical, emotional and sexual abuse as a result of being scapegoated as responsible for misfortunes and difficulties which occur in a family or within close networks. Witchcraft labelling of children results in neglectful and harmful parenting, particularly when allegations of witchcraft have been corroborated by a highly regarded person or persons within the community.

Figure 10.2   Witchcraft labelling: assessment, intervention and support

> We invite you to add to the wordle in Figure 10.2 from your reading of Awura Adjoa's narrative.
>
> Are there any words or phrases which overlap with Figure 10.1? Why might this be?

GOING FORWARD

We hope that this book, alongside extending our knowledge about witchcraft labelling, will also have prompted various professionals involved in child safeguarding to proactively consider when and how they might intervene when another child like Awura Adjoa presents themselves. We acknowledge that some of these recommendations may already be in place due to improved awareness and/or changes in legislation and policy in the UK; however, we have felt the need to restate them for emphasis.

Appendix 1 Witchcraft Labelling Assessment Framework (WLAF)

It is perhaps ambitious to attempt to provide a framework for assessing children and young people who may be at risk of witchcraft labelling; however, it feels like a useful way to end this book, not only having identified areas of risk and 'problems' but also offering suggestions about how assessments might be done. The current assessment frameworks are generic and are also dependant on social workers and other professionals being able to ask the right questions and generate data which will inform their assessments. The DfE (2007) provided a useful starting point in their non-statutory guidance *Safeguarding Children from Abuse Linked to a Belief in Spirit Possession* in which they reiterated the government's commitment to achieving the five key outcomes from their Every Child Matters, Change for Children Agenda.

While this provides a pragmatic framework for understanding this form of abuse, the absence of a practical tool for childcare practitioners to use in their daily interactions with families is unfortunate. It must be stated that although the ECM is no longer government policy, it provides some useful concepts for working with Awura Adjoa.

Notwithstanding, AFRUCA (2009) provides a range of resources about witchcraft-related abuse aimed at childcare practitioners and continue to work with individuals and groups from the African community. There have been other voluntary sector organisations – the Victoria Climbié Foundation (VCF), the Congolese Family Organisation – which also focus on work in this area.

The framework being proposed, WLAF, draws upon existing models of good practice in forming and maintaining relationships, culturally competent practice and assessing risk and vulnerability.

Below are ten questions and areas for consideration when assessing children and families where witchcraft labelling is suspected.

1. What are the presenting issues and how is the family describing these?
2. What are the family's beliefs (religious or otherwise)?
3. How long has the family had these beliefs and what have they said is the source of the beliefs?
4. How do these beliefs present in the day-to-day lives and functioning of the family? Ask the family to share some specific examples.
5. Do the family attend church or any other religious ceremonies – how often, where, and why? (This enables the practitioner to understand whether the family are attending a registered premise, or utilising 'house-churches' [Woods, 2013] as this might identify safeguarding concerns for children.)

6. Does the church or faith group believe in exorcism? Who can be exorcised and how is this performed?

7. Is the family affiliated to any community-based organisations or agencies? What do these organisations do and what is the nature of their affiliation?

8. Does the family understand safeguarding and the protection of children from a UK perspective?

9. Speak to the child on their own wherever possible and use an interpreter where required.

10. When speaking with the child, use language/terminology used by the parent/carer to create consistency and also to ensure accuracy of your analysis and conclusions.

Appendix 2 List of relevant voluntary and independent organisations

Africans Unite Against Child Abuse (AFRUCA), London and Manchester

www.afruca.org

Victoria Climbié Foundation (VCF)

www.vcf-uk.org

Churches' Child Protection Advisory Service (CCPAS)

www.ccpas.co.uk

National Society for the Prevention of Cruelty to Children (NSPCC)

www.nspcc.org.uk

Foundation for Women's Health Research and Development (FORWARD)

www.forwarduk.org.uk

Shika Tamaa Support Services (STASS)

www.stass.org.uk

Children and Families across Borders

www.cfab.org.uk

International Social Services

www.iss-ssi.org

TWITTER

B-MAG: @safeguardingBME

L J Hamblin-Opaluwa: @NoCHILD_WITCHES

Leethen Bartholomew: @leelenth

AFRUCA: @afruca

Appendix 3 Checklist for faith groups, churches and members

- Do you know the local authority (and relevant safeguarding teams) responsible for the area where your church is located?
- Does your church/faith group have a safeguarding policy?
- Have you appointed a safeguarding officer/lead (someone who is in charge of DBS checks and other suitability checks and investigations)?
- Do you deliver or provide regular training on safeguarding for the whole congregation and for lead members of the church/group? How often?
- Do your lead members know which 'sub-groups' and committees have been created? Who oversees these groups and how have safeguarding principles been embedded into their terms of reference?
- How does your church induct/welcome new members to the church?
- Does it include a discussion about safeguarding and other welfare-related issues?
- Do your processes and procedures clarify parents' and children's responsibilities and roles, especially in regard to fasting, deliverance, exorcism, for example?
- Is there a person nominated to take the lead in supporting members at external meetings and reviews (eg child welfare concerns, local authority and local education authority investigations and interventions)?
- Does your church/faith group hold formal meetings/prayer sessions/training in members' homes? If so, do you have safeguarding polices governing these activities?
- Is the lead pastor/elder accountable to a board or committee of some description?
- Does your church/faith group provide regular information and updates to its members about new legislation and other relevant information?
- Is your church/faith group affiliated to any safeguarding organisations in the voluntary sector?
- Are the messages given to church/faith group members consistent about the importance of safeguarding children, young people and vulnerable adults?

References

Adewuya, A O and Oguntade, A A (2007) Doctors' Attitudes towards People with Mental Illness in Western Nigeria. *Social Psychiatry Epidemiology*, 42: 931–6.

Adinkrah, M (2004) Witchcraft accusations and female homicide victimization in contemporary Ghana. *Violence Against Women*, 10(4): 325–56.

Adinkrah, M (2011) Child Witch Hunts in Contemporary Ghana. *Child Abuse and Neglect*, 35(9), 741–52.

AFRUCA (2009) *What is Witchcraft Abuse? Safeguarding African Children in the UK Series 5.* [online] Available at: www.afruca.org/wp-content/uploads/2013/06/SACUS05_What-is-witchcraft-abuse.pdf (accessed 21 March 2017).

AFRUCA (2014) *An Evaluation of the Dove Project.* London: TSIP. [online] Available at: www.afruca.org/wp-content/uploads/2015/01/Dove-Report-Evaluation-FINAL-with-logos.pdf (accessed 9 January 2017).

Agbanusi, A (2016) Witchcraft in West African Belief System – Medical and Social Dimensions. *Mgbakoigba: Journal of African Studies*, 5(2): 116–22.

Ainsworth, M D S (1979) Infant-mother Attachment. *American Psychologist*, 34: 932–7.

Akhtar, F (2013) *Mastering Social Work Values and Ethics.* London: Jessica Kingsley Publishers.

Akilapa, R and Simkiss, D (2012) Cultural Influences and Safeguarding Children. *Paediatrics and Child Health*, 22(11): 490–5.

Allain, L (2007) An Investigation of How a Group of Social Workers Respond to the Cultural Needs of Black Minority Ethnic Looked After Children. *Practice: Social Work In Action*, 9(2): 127–41.

Alston, P (2009, 27 May) Protection and Promotion of All Human Rights, Civil, Political, Economical, Social and Cultural Right, Including the Right to Development. *Report of the Special Rapporteur on Extrajudicial, Summary or Arbitrary Executions to the UN General Assembly*, A/HCR/11/2. New York.

Altomare, E, Vondra J I and Rubinstein, E (2005). Maternal Negative Affect and Perceptions of "Problem Children" in the Family. *Child Psychiatry and Human Development*, 35: 203–25.

Al-Zaben, F N and Sehlo, M G (2015) Punishment for Bedwetting Is Associated with Child Depression and Reduced Quality of Life. *Child Abuse & Neglect*, 34: 22–9.

Anghel, R and Ramon, S (2009) Service Users and Carers' Involvement in Social Work Education: Lessons from an English Case Study. *European Journal of Social Work*, 12(2): 185–99.

Arkell, H (2014) Ritual child abuse linked to witchcraft on the rise in the UK: Drownings and rape part of 'hidden crimes to drive out the devil'. *MailOnline*, 8 October 2014. [online] Available at: www.dailymail.co.uk/news/article-2784726/Ritual-child-abuse-linked-witchcraft-rise-UK-Drownings-rape-hidden-crimes-drive-devil.html#ixzz4cMwOkPFc (accessed 25 March 2017).

Asamoah-Gyadu, J K (2015) Witchcraft Accusations and Christianity in Africa. *International Bulletin of Missionary Research*, 39(1): 23–7.

Bahunga, J (2013) Tackling Child Abuse Linked to Faith or Belief. *Every Child Journal*, 3(3): 14–19. [online] Available at: www.afruca.org/wp-content/uploads/2013/07/ECJ-3-4-Faith-based-abuse.pdf (accessed 6 February 2017).

Barn, R and Kirton, D (2016) Safeguarding Black Children: An Exploration of Physical Abuse, in Bernard, C and Harris, P (eds) *Safeguarding Black Children: Good Practice in Child Protection.* London: Jessica Kingsley Publishers.

Bartholomew, L (2015) Child Abuse Linked to Beliefs in Witchcraft. *Transnational Social Review*, 5(2): 193–8.

Baumeister, R (2005) Rejected and Alone. *The Psychologist*, 18(12): 732–5.

BBC (2013) Child 'training' book triggers backlash. [online] Available at: www.bbc.co.uk/news/magazine-25268343 (accessed 10 January 2017).

Becker, H S (1991, orig. 1966) *Outsiders: Studies in the Sociology of Deviance*. New York: Simon and Schuster.

Beddoe, E, Davys, A M and Adamson, C (2014) 'Never Trust Anybody Who Says "I Don't Need Supervision"': Practitioners' Beliefs about Social Worker Resilience. *Practice*, 26(2): 113–30.

Bernard, C and Gupta, A (2008) Black African Children and the Child Protection System. *British Journal of Social Work*, 38, 476–92.

Bernard, C and Harris, P (eds) (2016) *Safeguarding Black Children: Good Practice in Child Protection*. London: Jessica Kingsley Publishers.

Bledsoe, C H and Sow, P (2011) Back to Africa: Second Chances for the Children of West African Immigrants. *Journal of Marriage and Family*, 73(4): 747–62.

Bolton, G (2006) Narrative Writing: Reflective Enquiry into Professional Practice. *Educational Action Research*, 14(2): 203–18.

Botham, J (2011) The Complexities of Children Missing from Education: A Local Project to Address the Health Needs of School-aged Children. *Community Practitioner*, 84(5): 31–4.

Bottoms, B L, Shaver, P R, Goodman, G S and Qin, J (1995) In the Name of God: A Profile of Religion-related Child Abuse. *Journal of Social Issues*, 51(2): 85–111.

Bourdieu, P (1991) *Language and Symbolic Power*. Oxford: Polity.

Bowlby, J (1969) *Attachment and Loss* (vol 1). New York: Basic Books.

Brammer, A (2015) *Social Work Law* (4th ed). Harlow: Pearson.

Briggs, S, Whittaker, A, Linford, H, Bryan, A, Ryan, E and Ludick, D (2011) *Safeguarding Children's Rights: Exploring Issues of Witchcraft and Spirit Possession in London's African Communities*. London: Trust for London and Centre for Social Work Research.

British Association of Social Workers (BASW) (2012) *The Code of Ethics for Social Work: Statement of Principles*. [online] Available at: http://cdn.basw.co.uk/upload/basw_95243-9.pdf (accessed 21 March 2017).

British Association of Social Workers (BASW) (2014) *Professional Capabilities Framework*. [online] Available at: www.basw.co.uk/pcf/ (accessed 21 March 2017).

Broadhurst, K, Paton, H and May-Chalal, C (2005) Children Missing from School Systems: Exploring Divergent Patterns of Disengagement in the Narrative Accounts of Parents, Carers, Children and Young People. *British Journal of Sociology of Education*, 26(1): 105–19.

Canda, E R and Furman, L D (2009) *Spiritual Diversity in Social Work Practice: The Heart of Helping*. New York: Oxford University Press.

Cavendish, R (1994) *The World of Ghosts and the Supernatural*. New York: Facts on File Inc.

Chaudhury, S (2012) Women as Easy Scapegoats: Witchcraft Accusations and Women as Targets in Tea Plantations of India. *Violence against Women*, 18(10): 1213–34.

Cimpric, A. (2010) *Children Accused of Witchcraft. An Anthropological Study of Contemporary Practices in Africa*. UNICEF. [online] Available at: www.unicef.org/wcaro/wcaro_children-accused-of-witchcraft-in-Africa.pdf (accessed 10 January 2017).

Clandinin, D J (2007) Preface, in Clandinin, D J (ed), *Handbook of Narrative Inquiry: Mapping a Methodology*. Thousand Oaks, CA: Sage Publications, Inc, pp ix–xvii.

Clandinin, D J and Connelly, F M (2000) *Narrative Inquiry: Experience and Story in Qualitative Research*. San Francisco: Jossey-Bass Publishers.

Cohan, J A (2011) The Problem of Witchcraft Violence in Africa. *Suffolk University Law Review*, 44(4): 803–72.

Connolly, M, Crichton-Hill, Y and Ward, T (2006) *Culture and Child Protection: Reflexive Responses.* London: Jessica Kingsley Publishing.

Coulshed, V and Orme, J (2006) *Social Work Practice* (4th ed). London: Palgrave Macmillan.

Crisp, B, Anderson, M R and Orme, J (2003) *Learning and Teaching Assessment Skills in Social Work Education. SCIE Knowledge Review.* London: Social Care Institute for Excellence.

Cummins, J and Miller, C (2007) *Co-production, Social Capital and Service Effectiveness.* PMO: London.

Cunningham, J and Cunningham, S (2008) *Sociology and Social Work.* Exeter: Learning Matters.

Davies, L and Duckett, N (2016) *Proactive Child Protection and Social Work* (2nd ed). London: Learning Matters/Sage.

Department for Children, Schools and Families (DCSF) (2010) *Safeguarding Children and Young People Who May Be Affected by Gang Activity.* London: HMSO.

Department for Education (DfE) (2006) *Working Together to Safeguard Children: A Guide to Inter-agency Working to Safeguard and Promote the Welfare of Children.* London: HMSO.

Department for Education (DfE) (2014) *Knowledge and Skills for Child and Family Social Work.* [online] Available at: http://cdn.basw.co.uk/upload/basw_114911-5.pdf (accessed 23 March 2017).

Department for Education (DfE) (2015) *Working Together to Safeguard Children: A Guide to Inter-agency Working to Safeguard and Promote the Welfare of Children.* London: HMSO.

Department for Education (DfE) (2016a) *Children Missing Education: Statutory Guidance for Local Authorities.* London: HMSO. [online] Available at: www.gov.uk/government/uploads/system/uploads/attachment_data/file/550416/Children_Missing_Education_-_statutory_guidance.pdf (accessed 6 February 2017).

Department for Education (DfE) (2016b) *Keeping Children Safe in Education: Statutory Guidance for Schools and Colleges.* [online] Available at: www.gov.uk/government/uploads/system/uploads/attachment_data/file/550511/Keeping_children_safe_in_education.pdf (accessed 21 March 2017).

Department for Education (DfE) (2016c) *Wood Report: Review of the Role and Functions of Local Safeguarding Children Boards.* [online] Available at: www.gov.uk/government/uploads/system/uploads/attachment_data/file/526329/Alan_Wood_review.pdf (accessed 23 March 2017).

Department for Education and Skills (DfES) (2004) *Every Child Matters.* London: HMSO. [online] Available at: www.gov.uk/government/uploads/system/uploads/attachment_data/file/272064/5860.pdf (accessed 21 March 2017).

Department for Education and Skills (DfES) (2007) *Safeguarding Children from Abuse Linked to a Belief in Spirit Possession.* London. HMSO.

Department of Health (DoH) (2000) *Assessing Children in Need and their Families: Practice Guidance.* London: HMSO. [online] Available at: http://dera.ioe.ac.uk/15599/1/assessing_children_in_need_and_their_families_practice_guidance_2000.pdf (accessed 22 March 2017).

Dioum, M and Yorath, S (2013) Safeguarding Vulnerable Children: The Role of the Victoria Climbié Foundation. *Journal of Health Visiting*, 1(2): 80–5.

Dominelli, L and McLeod, E (1989) *Feminist Social Work.* Basingstoke: Macmillan Education.

Dotti Sani, G M (2016) Undoing Gender in Housework? Participation in Domestic Chores by Italian Fathers and Children at Different Ages. *Sex Roles*, 74: 411–21.

Douglas, M (1970) (ed) *Witchcraft Confessions and Accusations.* London: Tavistock.

Doyle, C and Timms, C (2014) *Child Neglect & Emotional Abuse: Understanding, Assessment & Response.* London: Sage.

Doyle, C, Timms, C D and Sheehan, E (2010) Potential Sources of Support for Children Who Have Been Emotionally Abused by Parents. *Vulnerable Children and Youth Studies*, 5(3): 230–43.

Ellis, J (1977) Differing Conceptions of a Child's Needs: Some Implications for Social Work with West African Children and Their Parents. *British Journal of Social Work*, 7: 156–71.

Erikson, E (1995) *Childhood and Society*. Norton: New York.

Felker, B (2007) Spanking Away Sin. *The Christian Century*, 124(9): 8–9.

Figueira-McDonough, J, Ellen Netting, F and Nichols-Casebolt, A (2001) Subjugated Knowledge in Gender-Integrated Social Work Education: Call for Dialogue. *AFFILIA*, 16(4): 411–31.

Finch, J, Schaub, J and Dalrymple, R (2013) Projective Identification and the Fear of Failing: Making Sense of Practice Educators' Experiences of Failing Social Work Students in Practice Learning Settings. *Journal of Social Work Practice: Psychotherapeutic Approaches in Health, Welfare and the Community*, 28(2): 1–16.

Fook, J (1999) Reflexivity as Method. In Daley, J, Kellahear, A and Willis, E (eds) *Annual Review of Health Social Sciences*, 9: 11–20.

Furness, S and Gilligan, P (2010) *Religion, Beliefs and Social Work: Making a Difference*. Social Work in Practice Series. Bristol: Policy Press.

Gershman, B (2015) Witchcraft Beliefs and the Erosion of Social Capital: Evidence from Sub-Saharan Africa and Beyond. *Journal of Development Economics*, 120: 182–208.

Gilligan, P (2009) Considering Religion and Beliefs in Child Protection and Safeguarding Work: Is Any Consensus Emerging? *Child Abuse Review*, 18: 94–110.

Goddard, C (2012) Behind closed doors. [online] Available at: www.cypnow.co.uk/cyp/fea-ture/1071803/behind-closed-doors (accessed 21 March 2017).

Godina, L (2012) Religion and Parenting: Ignored Relationship? *Child and Family Social Work*, 19(4): 381–90.

Goffman, E (1963) *Stigma: Notes on the Management of Spoiled Identity*. Englewood Cliffs, NJ: Prentice-Hall.

Hall, H (2016) Exorcism, Religious Freedom and Consent: The Devil in the Detail. *The Journal of Criminal Law*, 80(4): 241–53.

Hanisch, D and Moulding, N (2011) Power, Gender, and Social Work Responses to Child Sexual Abuse. *Afflia: Journal of Women and Social Work*, 26(3): 278–90.

Harper, L J (2016) Supporting Young Children's Transitions to School: Recommendations for Families. *Early Childhood Education Journal*, 44: 653–59.

Hauari, H and Hollingworth, H (2009) *Understanding Fathering: Masculinity, Diversity and Change*. London: Joseph Rowntree Foundation [online] Available at: www.jrf.org.uk/report/understanding-fathering-masculinity-diversity-and-change (accessed 23 March 2017).

Health Care Professions Council (HCPC online) (2017) *Standards of Proficiency for Social Workers in England*. [online] Available at: www.hpc-uk.org/assets/documents/10003b08standardsofproficiency-social workersinengland.pdf (accessed 21 March 2017).

Hermkens, A K (2015) The Gendered Politics of Witchcraft and Sorcery Accusations among Maisin of Papua New Guinea. *The Asia Pacific Journal of Anthropology*, 16(1): 36–54.

Hjelm, K and Mufunda, E (2010) Zimbabwean Diabetics' Beliefs about Health and Illness: An Interview Study. *BMC International Health and Human Rights*, 10(7): 2–10.

Hooper, C A and Warwick, I (2006) Gender and the Politics of Service Provision for Adults with a History of Childhood Sexual Abuse. *Critical Social Policy*, 26: 467–79.

Horwath, J and Lees, J (2010) Assessing the Influence of Religious Beliefs and Practices, on Parenting Capacity: The Challenges for Social Work Practitioners. *British Journal of Social Work*, 40: 82–99.

Humphrey, C (2015) Evil, Child Abuse and the Caring Professions. *Journal of Religion and Health*, 54: 1660–71.

International Federation of Social Workers (IFSW) (2014) Global definition for social work. [online] Available at: http://ifsw.org/get-involved/global-definition-of-social-work/ (accessed 21 March 2017).

International Social Services (ISS) (2017) Cross border protection. [online] Available at: http://iss-ssi.org/index.php/en/what-we-do-en/mediation-en (accessed 23 March 2017).

Irvine, J, Molyneux, J and Gillman, M (2015) 'Providing a Link with the Real World': Learning from the Student Experience of Service User and Carer Involvement in Social Work Education. *Social Work Education*, 34(2): 138–50.

Jones, D (2010) Assessment of Parenting, in Horwath, J (ed) *The Child's World*. London: Jessica Kingsley.

Joyce, K (2013) Return to Sender: Hundreds of Evangelical Families Thought They Were Bringing God's Word to Kids from War-torn Countries–by Adopting Them. And Then Reality Set In. *Mother Jones*, May–June 2013: 46–54.

Keeble, H and Hollington, K (2011) *Hidden Victims: The Real Story of Britain's Vulnerable Children and the People Who Rescue Them*. London: Simon and Schuster.

Kline, P M, McMackin, R and Lezotte, E (2008) The Impact of the Clergy Abuse Scandal on Parish Communities. *Journal of Child Sexual Abuse*, 17(3–4): 290–300.

Kotchick, B A and Forehand, R (2002) Putting Parenting in Perspective: A Discussion of the Contextual Factors That Shape Parenting Practices. *Journal of Child and Family Studies*, 11(3): 255–69.

La Fontaine, J S (ed) (2009) *The Devil's Children: From Spirit Possession to Witchcraft*. Farnham: Ashgate.

Laird, S (2008) *Anti-Oppressive Social Work: A Guide for Developing Cultural Competence*. London: Sage.

Lamb, M (ed) (1986) *The Father's Role: Applied Perspectives*. New York: John Wiley & Sons.

Laming, H (2003) *The Victoria Climbié Inquiry*. London: HMSO.

Levack, B P (2014) The Horrors of Witchcraft and Demonic Possession. *Social Research: An International Quarterly*, 81(4): 921–39.

Linards, J (2011) Baptismal Exorcism: An Exercise in Liturgical Theology. *Lutheran Theological Journal*, 45(3): 183–97.

Link, B G and Phelan, J C (2001) Conceptualising Stigma. *Annual Review of Sociology*, 27: 363–85.

Link, B G, Yang, L H, Phelan, J C and Collins, P Y (2004) Measuring Mental Illness Stigma. *Schizophrenia Bulletin*, 30(3): 511–41.

Maclean, S (2016) Whatever the Weather: A New Model for Critical Reflection. *Professional Social Work*, March: 28–29.

Martin, R (2011) *Social Work Assessment*. Exeter: Learning Matters.

Maslow, A H (1970) *Motivation and Personality* (2nd ed). New York: Harper and Row.

Mather, M and Kerac, M (2002) Caring for the Health of Children Brought to the UK from Abroad. *Adoption and Fostering*, 26(4): 44–54.

Mathews, I (2009) *Social Work and Spirituality*. Exeter: Learning Matters.

May, V (2011) Self, Belonging and Social Change. *Sociology*, 45(3): 363–78.

Mays, V M (2000) A Social Justice Agenda. *American Psychologist*, 55: 326–7.

Mazzucato, V, Cebotari, V, Veale, A, White, A, Grassi, M and Vivet, J (2015) International Parental Migration and the Psychological Wellbeing of children in Ghana and Nigeria. *Social Science & Medicine*, 132: 215–24.

Mercer, J (2012) Deliverance, Demonic Possession and Mental Illness. *Mental Health, Religion and Culture*, 16(6): 595–611.

Merolla, D and Jackson, O (2014) Understanding Differences in College Enrollment: Race, Class and Cultural Capital. *Race and Social Problems*, 6: 280–92.

Moore, M J C and Buehler, C (2011) Parents' Divorce Proneness: The Influence of Adolescent Problem Behaviours and Parental Efficacy. *Journal of Social and Personal Relationships*, 28(5): 634–52.

Moore, M R (2008) Gendered Power Relations among Women: A Study of Household Decision Making in Black, Lesbian Stepfamilies. *American Sociological Review*, 73(2): 335–6.

Moss, P, Clark, A and Kjorholt, A T (eds) (2005) *Beyond Listening: Children's Perspectives on Early Childhood Services*. Bristol: Policy Press.

Munro, E and Hubbard, A (2011) A Systems Approach to Evaluating Organisational Change in Children's Social Care. *The British Journal of Social Work*, 41(4): 726–43.

Niehaus, I (2013) Aids, Speech and Silence in South Africa. *Anthropology Today*, 29(3): 8–12.

Nzira, V (2011) *Social Care with African Families in the UK*. London: Routledge.

O'Carroll, V, McSwiggan, L and Campbell, M (2016) Health and Social Care Professionals' Attitudes to Interprofessional Working and Interprofessional Education: A Literature Review. *Journal of Interprofessional Care*, 30(1): 42–9.

Obadina, S (2012) Witchcraft Accusations and Exorcisms: A Form of Child Abuse. *British Journal of School Nursing*, 7(6): 287–91.

Ochieng, B M N (2003) Minority Ethnic Families and Family Centred Care. *Journal of Child Health Care*, 7(2): 123–32.

Padilla-Walker, L M and Thompson, R A (2005) Combatting Conflicting Messages of Values: A Closer Look at Parental Strategies. *Social Development*, 14(2): 305–23.

Pargament, K I (1997) *The Psychology of Religion and Coping: Theory, Research, Practice*. New York: The Guilford Press.

Parke, R D (2013) *Future Families: Diverse Forms, Rich Possibilities*. Malden, MA: Wiley.

Parker, J and Bradley, G (2010) *Social Work Practice: Assessment, Planning, Intervention and Review* (3rd ed). Exeter: Learning Matters.

Pearl, M and Pearl, D (2009) *To Train Up a Child: Turning the Hearts of the Fathers to the Children*. Pleasantville, TN: No Greater Joy Ministries Inc. (E-Book).

Pearson, J (2010) Resisting Rhetorics of Violence: Women, Witches and Wicca. *Feminist Theology*, 18(2): 141–59.

Peng, Y and Wong, O M H (2016) Who Takes Care of My Left-behind Children? Migrant Mothers and Caregivers in Transnational Child Care. *Journal of Family Issues*, 37(4): 2021–44.

Pitcher, D and Arnill, M (2010) 'Allowed to be There': The Wider Family and Child Protection. *Practice*, 22(1): 17–31.

Redsell, S A and Collier, J (2000) Bedwetting, Behaviour and Self-esteem: A Review of the Literature. *Child, Care, Health and Development*, 27(2): 149–62.

Remenyi, D (2012) *Case Study Research*, edited by Dan Remenyi. Academic Conferences Publishing International. ProQuest Ebook Central. [online] Available at: https://books.google.co.uk/books?hl=en&lr=&id=xMsRBAAAQBAJ&oi=fnd&pg=PR7&ots=lHlhflCi0b&sig=S73eA57CgG-QsOV46BS75Mqwl5Q#v=onepage&q&f=false (accessed 23 March 2017).

Robinson, L (2007) *Cross-cultural Child Development for Social Workers: An Introduction*. Basingstoke: Palgrave MacMillan.

Rodriguez, C M and Henderson, R C (2010) Who Spares the Rod? Religious Orientation, Social Conformity and Child Abuse Potential. *Child Abuse and Neglect*, 39: 84–94.

Roose, R and De Bie, M (2008) Children's Rights: A Challenge for Social Work. *International Social Work*, 51(1): 37–46.

Schulkind, M, Schoppel, K and Scheiderer, E (2012) Gender Differences in Autobiographical Narratives: He Shoots and Scores; She Evaluates and Interprets. *Memory & Cognition*, 40(6): 958–65.

Sheikh, A (2005) Jinn and Cross-cultural Care. *Journal of the Royal Society of Medicine*, 98(8): 339–40.

Skills for Care (2016) *Social Work Education in England*. [online] Available at: www.nmds-sc-online.org.uk/Get.aspx?id=995424 (accessed 24 January 2017).

Stabell, T D (2010) 'The Modernity of Witchcraft' and the Gospel in Africa. *Missiology: An International Review*, 38(4): 460–74.

Statham, J and Chase, E (2010) *Childhood Wellbeing: A Brief Overview*. Childhood Wellbeing Research Centre. [online] Available at: www.gov.uk/government/uploads/system/uploads/attachment_data/file/183197/Child-Wellbeing-Brief.pdf (accessed 20 February 2017).

Stobart, E (2006) Child Abuse Linked to Accusations of 'Possession' and 'Witchcraft'. Research Report 750. London: Department for Education and Skills, pp 151–72. [online] Available at: http://dera.ioe.ac.uk/6416/1/RR750.pdf (accessed 23 March 2017).

Stone, C (2016) Fostering Emotional Intelligence Within Social Work Practice, in Stone, C and Harbin, F (eds) *Transformative Learning for Social Work: Learning For and In Practice*. London: Palgrave.

Streets, F (2009) Overcoming a Fear of Religion in Social Work Education and Practice. *Journal of Religion & Spirituality in Social Work: Social Thought*, 28: 1–2, 185–99.

Tedam, P (2013) Developing Cultural Competence, in Bartoli, A (ed) *Anti-racism in Social Work Practice*. St Albans: Critical Publishing.

Tedam, P (2014) Witchcraft Branding and the Abuse of African Children in the UK: Causes, Effects and Professional Intervention. *Early Childhood Development and Care*, 184(9–10): 1403–14.

Tedam, P (2016) Safeguarding Children at Risk of Witchcraft Accusations, in Bernard, C and Harris, P (eds) *Safeguarding Black Children*. London. Jessica Kingsley Publishers.

Ter Haar, G (ed) (2007) *Imagining Evil: Witchcraft Beliefs and Accusations in Contemporary Africa*. Asmara, NJ: Africa World Press.

Thompson, N and Pascal, J (2012) Developing Critically Reflective Practice. *Reflective Practice*, 13(2): 311–25.

Trevithick, P (2005) *Social Work Skills: A Practice Handbook*. Maidenhead: Open University Press.

Triandis, H C (1995) *Individualism & Collectivism: New Directions in Social Psychology*. Boulder: Westview Press.

Tsui, M (2005) *Social Work Supervision: Contexts and Concepts*. London: Sage.

Tucker, E and Maunder, R (2015) Helping Children Get Along: Teachers' Strategies for Dealing with Bullying in Primary Schools. *Educational Studies*, 41(4): 466–70.

Twum-Danso Imoh, A (2012) Cultural Practices in the Face of Globalized Ideals: The Case of Physical Punishment of Children in Ghana, in Twum-Danso Imoh, A and Ame, R (eds) *Childhoods at the Intersection of the Local and Global*. Basingstoke: Palgrave.

UN Convention on the Rights of the Child (1990) Preamble. [online] Available at: www.un.by/en/hr/doc/child/ (accessed 21 March 2017).

Verhoef, H (2005) A Child Has Many Mothers: Views of Child Fostering in Northwestern Cameroon. *Childhood*, 12: 369–90.

Walker, S D (2005) *Culturally Competent Therapy: Working with Children and Young People*. London: Palgrave Macmillan.

Walker, S D (2012) *Effective Social Work with Children, Young People and Families: Putting Systems Theory into Practice*. London: Sage.

Weekes-Barnard, D (2010) *Did They Get It Right? A Re-examination of School Exclusions and Race Equality.* London: Runnymede Trust.

Wilkins, D and Boahen, G (2013) *Critical Analysis Skills for Social Workers.* Maidenhead: Open University Press.

Wolfgang, B (2004) *Witches and Witch-hunts: A Global History.* Cambridge: Polity Press.

Woods, O (2013) Converting Houses into Churches: The Mobility, Fission, and Sacred Networks of Evangelical House Churches in Sri Lanka. *Environment and Planning D: Society and Space*, 31: 1062–75.

Yardley, M (2008) Social Work Practice with Pagans, Witches, and Wiccans: Guidelines for Practice with Children and Youths. *Social Work*, 53(4): 329–36.

Yin, R K (2010) *Qualitative Research from Start to Finish.* London: Guilford Press.

Index